# MY PRAYER BOOK

# My Prayer Book

## A New Manual of Prayers and Devotions

REV. GEORGE J. RYAN
REV. VICTOR HOAGLAND, C.P.
Editors

THE REGINA PRESS
New York

*Nihil Obstat:*   Otto L. Garcia, j.c.d.
                Diocesan Censor

*Imprimatur:*   Francis J. Mugavero, d.d.
                Bishop of Brooklyn, N.Y.

*Date:*           November 24, 1981

© 1981 by Regina Press, New York

Excerpts from the English translation of *Rite of Penance* © 1974, International Committee on English in the Liturgy, Inc. (ICEL); excerpts from the English translation of *Rite of Penance: Appendix III, Form of Examination of Conscience* © 1975, ICEL. All rights reserved.

**Excerpts from *The Jerusalem Bible*, copyright © 1966 by Darton, Longman & Todd, Ltd. and Doubleday & Company, Inc. Used by permission of the publisher.**

ISBN 0-88271-041-9

# Table of Contents

| | |
|---|---|
| Introduction | 9 |
| **Brief Statement of Christian Doctrine** | 11 |
| The Core of Christian Faith | 12 |
| The Sacraments | 13 |
| The Beatitudes | 14 |
| The Corporal and Spiritual Works of Mercy | 15 |
| The Ten Commandments | 17 |
| The Greatest Commandment of All | 18 |
| Ecclesiastical Laws | 19 |
| Holy Days of Obligation | 22 |
| Fast and Abstinence | 22 |
| **Everyday Prayers** | 23 |
| Sign of the Cross | 24 |
| The Lord's Prayer | 24 |
| The Hail Mary | 25 |
| Glory Be to the Father | 25 |
| Grace Before Meals | 26 |
| Grace After Meals | 26 |
| Come Holy Spirit | 26 |
| Acts of Faith, Hope, Charity | 27 |
| The Apostles' Creed | 29 |
| The Confiteor | 30 |
| Act of Contrition | 30 |
| **Morning and Evening Prayer** | 31 |

| | |
|---|---|
| **Prayers for the Liturgical Year** | 63 |
|    Advent | 64 |
|    Christmas | 66 |
|    Lent | 68 |
|    Easter | 70 |
|    Pentecost | 72 |
|    Prayer for Our Parish | 74 |
| **Prayers Before Communion** | 76 |
| **Prayers After Communion** | 83 |
| **The Sacrament of Reconciliation** | 91 |
| **Devotions to Our Lord in the Blessed Sacrament** | 105 |
| **Benediction of the Blessed Sacrament** | 115 |
| **Devotions to the Sacred Heart of Jesus** | 123 |
| **The Litanies** | 133 |
|    Sacred Heart of Jesus | 135 |
|    Most Holy Name of Jesus | 138 |
|    Blessed Virgin Mary | 142 |
|    St. Joseph | 146 |
|    The Saints | 149 |
| **Novenas** | 155 |
|    Our Lady of the Miraculous Medal | 157 |
|    Our Lady of Fatima | 160 |
|    Our Mother of Perpetual Help | 161 |
|    Our Lady of Lourdes | 162 |

| | |
|---|---|
| Our Lady of the Immaculate Conception | 164 |
| Our Lady of Guadalupe | 166 |
| Our Lady of Czestochowa | 168 |
| Our Lady of Mount Carmel | 169 |
| Sacred Heart of Jesus | 170 |
| Infant of Prague | 173 |
| St. Joseph | 175 |
| St. Anne | 177 |
| St. Anthony | 178 |
| St. Jude | 180 |
| St. Elizabeth Ann Seton | 181 |
| St. Theresa, the Little Flower | 182 |
| Rosary Novena | 184 |

## The Way of the Cross — 185

## Prayers to the Blessed Mother — 205

| | |
|---|---|
| The Regina Caeli | 206 |
| The Angelus | 207 |
| The Memorare | 208 |
| Prayer of St. Alphonsus Liguori | 209 |
| Prayer of St. Francis de Sales | 211 |
| Prayer of St. Louis de Montfort | 212 |
| Prayer of St. Thomas Aquinas | 213 |
| The Thirty Days' Prayer | 214 |

## The Rosary of the Blessed Virgin Mary — 221

## Devotion of the Five First Saturdays — 229

## Feasts of the Blessed Virgin Mary — 233

| | |
|---|---|
| Prayers to St. Joseph | 237 |
| Thanksgiving Prayers | 247 |
| Prayers for Peace | 253 |
| Special Prayers | 257 |
| Prayers of the Saints | 273 |
| The Universal Prayer | 281 |
| Prayer of the Heart | 284 |

# INTRODUCTION

"I'LL TELL YOU what is the great work you have to do all your life," said a saint long ago. "It's the work of prayer. You can stop everything else you do, every job or service you perform, but you can never stop praying. That is what scripture teaches: 'Pray always'."

Prayer is a person-to-person *communication* with God. One who prays converses, loves and relates to Him who has loved first. Our God has been revealed as Father, Son and Holy Spirit so in prayer we address and relate to three Persons as well as to those holy people who now share fully that divine life in glory.

Prayer can take various forms. But the organ and origin of all prayer is the 'heart', that deepest part of oneself created in the image and likeness of God. Prayer can be understood as a 'heart' that overflows with joy, thanksgiving, gratitude, praise and petition.

Sometimes words are not necessary for this prayer; other times they are its apt expression. This prayer book gives shape to those sentiments and hopefully will lead the way to a deeper and more conscious relationship with God.

This is a book of prayers to help you as you pray. Prayers for all seasons, and all occasions; prayers new and old. Some you may know already by heart; some you may welcome to see for the first time.

Many of the prayers in this book have their origin in the great traditional devotions of the Church. Inspired by the Holy Spirit, nourished by the holy lives and desires of countless faithful Christians, they come to help us in our turn to be a people close to our God. Like bread for the hungry, like water for the thirsting, prayer brings strength and peace to the hours of our day and the years of our life. Prayer at the same time is a personal response to God's **presence**. Thus, before saying any of the following prayers, let the one who prays acknowledge God's presence and then open his or her heart in words of faith, hope and love.

# Brief Statement of Christian Doctrine

# The Core of Christian Faith

YES, Jesus Christ is our Teacher and Lord. His life and words draw men and women of every age and nation to his side. No other great figure of history approaches what he said and did.

Born poor, his childhood spent in an obscure Galilaean village, he suddenly emerged for a few dazzling years to teach and work wonders in the Jewish world of his time.

He was opposed by those in power who brought him to trial and crucified him. After three days he rose from the dead.

Those who witnessed his rising from death told the good news to others. They were convinced he was the son of God who came to bring new life and hope to a world lost in darkness. He would bring a new kingdom, a new order, based on justice and love.

Jesus promised to remain always with his Church. Receiving his Holy Spirit, his Church would proclaim his life and words. Above all, they would offer the world his love.

# The Sacraments

THE CATHOLIC CHURCH seeks to remain one with Jesus Christ in a variety of ways. One of these is the sacraments —seven great signs that mark the different stages and events in human life. From birth till death, the follower of Jesus reaches out to him for power and life to love and live as he did. The sacraments are key events for Christ to draw men and women more fully into his saving actions. These ritual acts of human communication and human worship in the church are events of grace in which the Spirit of God is imparted by the Lord who is ever sending His Spirit into the world. Through the sacraments Jesus is always present to those who believe in him. They are:

>    Baptism
>    Confirmation
>    Eucharist
>    Reconciliation
>    Anointing of the Sick
>    Marriage
>    Holy Orders

# The Beatitudes

JESUS PROMISED happiness to those who believed in him and follow his teaching. He summed up his promises in his Sermon on the Mount. What he taught there, he lived himself and the stories and events of the New Testament re-echo these same central truths. The Beatitudes are a summary of the different directions in life that lead to the peace and happiness promised by Jesus. The traditional listing of the beatitudes is:

1. Blessed are the poor in spirit: the reign of God is theirs.

2. Blessed are the sorrowing: they shall be consoled.

3. Blessed are the lowly: they shall inherit the land.

4. Blessed are they who hunger and thirst for holiness: they shall have their fill.

5. Blessed are they who show mercy: mercy shall be theirs.

6. Blessed are the single-hearted: for they shall see God.

7. Blessed are the peacemakers: they shall be called sons of God.

8. Blessed are those persecuted for holiness' sake: the reign of God is theirs.

## The Works of Mercy

JESUS TOLD US to love one another as he loved us. His own life revealed his loving concern and compassion for the poor, the sick and the troubled. The lonely leper isolated from society, the blind man alone in his darkness, the frightened woman taken in adultery, the thief condemned to a cross found in him care, support, and strength. He advised those who would follow him to make their love as practical and selfless as his own. The corporal and spiritual works of mercy are guidelines for Christian love.

## The Corporal Works of Mercy

To feed the hungry.

To give drink to the thirsty.

To clothe the naked.

To visit and ransom the captives.

To shelter the homeless.

To visit the sick.

To bury the dead.

## The Spiritual Works of Mercy

To admonish sinners.

To instruct the ignorant.

To counsel the doubtful.

To comfort the sorrowful.

To bear wrongs patiently.

To forgive all injuries.

To pray for the living and the dead.

# The Ten Commandments

JESUS REAFFIRMED the law that Moses, inspired by God, gave to the Jewish people. He came, he said, not to destroy the law but to fulfill it. Through the centuries the Judeo-Christian moral code has become a basic guideline for human conduct.

The human family left to its own wisdom often pursues a course of violence and destruction. The human heart, whose ways are "torturous" according to the Prophet Jeremiah, is prone to contraction and selfishness. "Out of the human heart comes evil thoughts, murder, adultery, fornication, theft, false witness, slander." (Mt. 15, 19)

The Ten Commandments warn of human deception and at the same time point out the proper way for one to live. Following Jesus Christ means to follow their teaching.

1. I, the Lord, am your God. You shall not have other gods besides me.
2. You shall not take the name of the Lord, your God, in vain.

3. Remember to keep holy the Sabbath Day.

4. Honor your father and your mother.

5. You shall not kill.

6. You shall not commit adultery.

7. You shall not steal.

8. You shall not bear false witness against your neighbor.

9. You shall not covet your neighbor's wife.

10. You shall not covet anything that belongs to your neighbor.

## The Greatest Commandment of All

"But when the Pharisees heard that he had silenced the Sadducees they got together and, to disconcert him, one of them put a question, 'Master, which is the greatest commandment of the Law? Jesus said, 'You must love the

Lord your God with all your heart, with all your soul, and with all your mind. This is the greatest and the first commandment. The second resembles it: You must love your neighbor as yourself. On these two commandments hang the whole Law, and the Prophets also.' "

*Matt. 22:34-40*


## Ecclesiastical Laws

IT IS IN CHRIST that authority of the Church dwells. The laws of the Church and the legitimate commands of the pope and bishops are issued with the authority Christ gave to the Church for the good of the People of God. The bishops of each country generally list the most notable of special duties of Catholics as 'Precepts of the Church'. The Bishops of the United States have endorsed the following for their people. (Those traditionally mentioned as precepts of the Church are marked with an asterisk.)

1. To keep holy the day of the Lord's resurrection: to worship God by participating in Mass every Sunday and Holy Day of Obligation: * to avoid those activities that would hinder renewal of soul and body, e.g., needless work and business activities, unnecessary shopping, etc.

2. To lead a sacramental life: to receive Holy Communion frequently and the Sacrament of Penance regularly-minimally, to receive the Sacrament of Penance at least once a year (annual confession is obligatory only if serious sin is involved).*-minimally, to receive Holy Communion at least once a year, between the first Sunday of Lent and Trinity Sunday.

3. To study Catholic teaching in preparation for the Sacrament of

Confirmation, to be confirmed, and then to continue to study and advance the cause of Christ.

4. To observe the marriage laws of the Church: * to give religious training (by example and word) to one's children; to use parish schools and religious education programs.

5. To strengthen and support the Church: * one's own parish community and parish priests; the worldwide Church and the Holy Father.

6. To do penance, including abstaining from meat and fasting from food on the appointed days.*

7. To join in the missionary spirit and apostolate of the Church.

# Holy Days of Obligation in the United States

1. All Sundays of the year
2. January 1 - Solemnity of Mary, the Mother of God
3. Ascension Thursday - 40 days after Easter
4. August 15 - Assumption of the Blessed Virgin Mary
5. November 1 - All Saints' Day
6. December 8 - The Immaculate Conception
7. December 25 - Christmas Day

## Fast and Abstinence

The obligation to fast allows Catholics from ages 21-59 to have one full meal and two smaller meals during a day of fast. The obligation to abstain does not allow Catholics from the age of 14 and older to eat meat on days of abstinence.

Ash Wednesday and Good Friday are days of fast and abstinence, while all Fridays during Lent are days of abstinence. The regulations concerning fast and abstinence will vary from diocese to diocese.

# Everyday Prayers

# Sign of the Cross

In the name of the Father,
 and of the Son, ✝ and of the Holy Spirit. Amen.

# The Lord's Prayer

Our Father, who art in heaven,
 hallowed be thy name;
 thy kingdom come;
 thy will be done on earth as it
 is in heaven.
Give us this day our daily bread;
 and forgive us our trespasses
 as we forgive those who trespass
 against us;
 and lead us not into temptation,
 but deliver us from evil.
 Amen.

# The Hail Mary

Hail Mary, full of grace,
  the Lord is with thee.
Blessed art thou among women,
  and blessed is the fruit
  of thy womb, Jesus.
Holy Mary, Mother of God,
  pray for us sinners,
  now and at the hour of our death.
  Amen.

# Glory Be to the Father

Glory be to the Father, and to the Son,
  and to the Holy Spirit.
As it was in the beginning, is now and
  ever shall be, world without end.
  Amen.

## Grace Before Meals

Bless us, O Lord, and these your gifts
  which we are about to receive
  from your bounty,
  through Christ our Lord. Amen

## Grace After Meals

We give you thanks, Almighty God,
  for these and all your blessings;
  you live and reign for ever and ever.
  Amen.

## Come Holy Spirit

Come, Holy Spirit, fill the hearts
  of your faithful and
  kindle in them the fire of your love.
Send forth your Spirit, and they shall be
  created;

And you will renew the face of the earth.
O God,
   on the first Pentecost
   you instructed the hearts of those
   who believed in you
   by the light of the Holy Spirit;
   under the inspiration
   of the same Spirit,
   give us a taste
   for what is right and true
   and a continuing sense of his presence
   and power;
   through Jesus Christ our Lord.
   Amen.


## An Act of Faith

O God,
I firmly believe all the truths
   that you have revealed
   and that you teach us
   through your Church,
   for you are truth itself and
   can neither deceive nor be deceived.

## An Act of Hope

O God,
I hope with complete trust that you will give me,
 through the merits of Jesus Christ,
 all the necessary grace in this world
 and everlasting life
 in the world to come,
 for this is what you have promised
 and you always keep your promises.

## An Act of Charity

O God,
I love you with my whole heart above all things,
 because you are infinitely good;
 and for your sake I love my neighbor
 as I love myself.

# The Apostles' Creed

I believe in God, the Father almighty,
  Creator of heaven and earth.

I believe in Jesus Christ, his only Son,
  our Lord.
  He was conceived by the power of the
  Holy Spirit
  and born of the Virgin Mary.
  He suffered under Pontius Pilate,
  was crucified, died, and was buried.
  He descended to the dead.
  On the third day he rose again.
  He ascended into heaven,
  and is seated at the right hand of the
  Father.
  He will come again to judge the living
  and the dead.

I believe in the Holy Spirit,
  the holy catholic Church,
  the communion of saints,
  the forgiveness of sins,
  the resurrection of the body,
  and life everlasting.
                              Amen.

# The Confiteor

I confess to almighty God,
   and to you, my brothers and sisters,
   that I have sinned through my own fault,
   in my thoughts and in my words,
   in what I have done,
   and in what I have failed to do;
   and I ask blessed Mary, ever Virgin,
   all the angels and saints,
   and you, my brothers and sisters,
   to pray for me to the Lord our God.

# Act of Contrition

My God, I am sorry for my sins
   with all my heart.
In choosing to do wrong and
   failing to do good,
   I have sinned against you
   whom I should love above all things.
I firmly intend with your help
   to sin no more, to do penance and
   to avoid whatever leads me to sin.
   Amen.

# Morning and Evening Prayer

# MORNING PRAYER

Father, may all we do today be inspired by you and continue with your saving help.
Let our work always begin with your blessing and through you reach completion. Amen.

Lord God, You bring us to the beginning of this day.
By your guidance may we not fail today, but grant that all our thoughts, words and activity may be in accord with your will. Amen.

Lord of the morning, noon and evening, we pray:
Cast our darkness from our hearts and send us the light of your truth, so that we may be guided by you today and walk in your love.
We ask this through Christ our Lord. Amen.

# EVENING PRAYER

Almighty God, we thank you for bringing us safely to the end of this day. We offer you the work of our hands as a sacrifice before your sight. We make this prayer through Christ our Lord. Amen.

Father of mercy, may our hearts never waver from loving your law. Lead us on through the darkness to the dawning of eternal life. We ask this through Jesus Christ. Amen.

May he support us all the day long, till the shades lengthen and the evening comes and the busy world is hushed and the fever of life is over and our work is done—then in his mercy—may he give us a safe lodging and a holy rest and peace at last.

*John Henry Newman*

# Sunday Morning

God, you are my God, I am seeking you,
  my soul is thirsting for you,
  and my flesh is longing for you,
  a land parched, weary and waterless;
  I long to gaze on you in the Sanctuary,
  and to see your power and glory.

Your love is better than life itself,
  my lips will recite your praise;
  all my life I will bless you,
  in your name lift up my hands.
*Psalm 63*

Glory to the Father...


## Reading

Jesus said,
'Whoever drinks this water will get thirsty again; but anyone who drinks the water that I shall give will never be thirsty again: the water that I shall give will turn into a spring inside him,

welling up to eternal life.' 'Sir,' said the woman 'give me some of that water, so that I may never get thirsty...'

*John 4:14-15*

## Intercessions

Blessed are you, Lord Jesus, Savior of the world, for giving your life to save us,
—by your precious blood we are saved.

You promised living waters to those who seek the truth,
—give us that water to quench our thirst.

You sent disciples to announce the Good News to all people,
—sustain those who proclaim your word.

To those who carry your Cross today in anguish,
—grant patience and courage.

Our Father...

*(Morning Prayer, p. 32)*

## Sunday Evening

Yahweh is my shepherd, I lack nothing.

In meadows of green grass he lets me lie.
  To the waters of repose he leads me;
  there he revives my soul.

He guides me by paths of virtue for the
  sake of his name.

Though I pass through a gloomy valley,
  I fear no harm; beside me your rod
  and your staff are there, to hearten
  me.

You prepare a table before me under
  the eyes of my enemies; you anoint
  my head with oil, my cup brims over.

Ah, how goodness and kindness pursue
  me, every day of my life; my home,
  the house of Yahweh, as long as I live!
  *Psalm 23*

Glory to the Father...

## Reading

Jesus said,
'I am the good shepherd; I know my own and my own know me, just as the Father knows me and I know the Father; and I lay down my life for my sheep.'

*John 10:14-15*

## Intercessions

We bless you, Jesus Christ, our Shepherd, for the life you have given us this day,
 —we rejoice in your love.

Look with favor on the flock that bears your name,
 —let no one the Father has given you perish.

Guide your church in the way of your Truth,
 —by your Holy Spirit make her faithful.

Feed us at the table of your Word and your Bread,
 —that we may follow you forever.

Our Father...

*(Evening Prayer, p. 33)*

## Monday Morning

I say this prayer to you, Yahweh, for at daybreak you listen for my voice; and at dawn I hold myself in readiness for you, I watch for you.

*Psalm 5*

I lift my heart to you, O Lord, to be strengthened for this day. Be with me in all I do, my God; guide me in all my ways.

I will carry some burdens today; some trials will be mine. So I wait for your help, Lord, lest I stumble and fall.

I will do my work, Father, the work begun by your Son. He lives in me and I in him; may his work today be done.

Glory to the Father...

### Reading

Do to no one what you would not want done to you. Give your bread to those who are hungry, and your clothes to those who are naked. Ask advice of every wise person; never scorn any profitable advice. Bless the Lord God in everything; beg him to guide your ways and bring your paths and purposes to their end.

*Tobit 4:15a, 16a, 18a, 19*

### Intercessions

God of all kindness, bless your church,
 —make your people faithful to you.

Eternal Shepherd, look kindly on our Holy Father and all bishops,
 —grant them wisdom and courage.

Ruler of Nations, look kindly on those who govern,
 —guide them in the ways of peace.

Judge of the living and the dead, be merciful to our deceased brothers and sisters,
 —receive them into eternal joy.

Our Father... *(Morning Prayer, p. 32)*

## Monday Evening

Father in heaven,
  I lift my eyes to you
  and wait for your help.

I am your servant,
  entrusted with your gifts;
  I am yours alone.

I lift my eyes to you
  who dwell in heaven.
Like a faithful servant,
  I wish to do your bidding.

As the eyes of a good servant
  are on the master,
  so are our eyes on the Lord,
  our God, till he bless us.


Glory to the Father. . .

## Reading

Think of the love that the Father has lavished on us, by letting us be called God's children; and that is what we are. My dear people, we are already the children of God but what we are to be in the future has not yet been revealed; all we know is, that when it is revealed we shall be like him because we shall see him as he really is.

*1 John 3:1a-2*

## Intercessions

Lord, remember your church throughout the world,
—that your people may dwell in peace.

Lord, remember those we have met today,
—that they may receive your gifts.

Lord, remember all families,
—that they may live in harmony.

Lord, remember the sick and the dying,
—that they may have your joy.

Our Father...

*(Evening Prayer, p. 33)*

## Tuesday Morning

Teach us to count how few days we have
and so gain wisdom of heart.
*Psalm 90*

Help us do today the things that matter,
not to waste the time we have.

Yes, the moments we have are precious,
Lord, see that we count them dear.
Teach us to number our days aright.
Fill us this day with your kindness,
that we may be glad and rejoice all
the days of our life.

Glory to the Father...

### Reading

What we are waiting for is what he
promised: the new heavens and new
earth, the place where righteousness
will be at home. So then, my friends,
while you are waiting, do your best to

live lives without spot or stain so that he will find you at peace. Think of our Lord's patience as your opportunity to be saved.

*2 Peter 3:13-15a*

## Intercessions

Christ, our Guide, grant that today we may follow what you command,
—we humbly ask you.

Christ, our Guide, grant that today your life may grow within us,
—we humbly ask you.

Christ, our Guide, grant that today we may live in peace,
—we humbly ask you.

Christ, our Guide, grant that today we may not fall into sin,
—we humbly ask you.

Our Father...

*(Morning Prayer, p. 32)*

## Tuesday Evening

Yahweh, my heart has no lofty ambitions, my eyes do not look too high.

I am not concerned with great affairs or marvels beyond my scope.

Enough for me to keep my soul tranquil and quiet like a child in its mother's arms, as content as a child that has been weaned.

Israel, rely on Yahweh, now and for always!

*Psalm 131*

Glory to the Father...

### Reading

Blessed be the God and Father of our Lord Jesus Christ, a gentle Father and the God of all consolation, who comforts us in all our sorrows, so that we can offer others, in their sorrows, the consolation that we have received from God ourselves.

*2 Corinthians 1:3-4*

## Intercessions

Lord Jesus, intercede for us with your heavenly Father,
—despite our offenses, abide with us.

Lord Jesus, conqueror of death, strengthen our faith in your resurrection,
—in the stillness of night, abide with us.

Lord Jesus, image of the unseen God, help us to know the Father,
—in our works, abide with us.

Lord Jesus, light of the world, bring us hope that never fails,
—by your Spirit, abide with us.

Our Father...

*(Evening Prayer, p. 33)*

# Wednesday Morning

Praise Yahweh, my soul! I mean to
  praise Yahweh all my life, I mean to
  sing to my God as long as I live.
                              *Psalm 146*

Praise the Lord, my mind and memory,
  my thoughts and deeds of this day.
  I will praise the Lord wherever I go;
  I will sing praise, for the Lord is good.

Praise the Lord, strangers and friends;
  let us praise him for he loves us;
  let us sing praise to our God while
  we live.

Glory to the Father...

## Reading

Love is always patient and kind; it is
never jealous; love is never boastful or
conceited; it is never rude or selfish; it
does not take offence, and is not

resentful. Love takes no pleasure in other people's sins but delights in the truth; it is always ready to excuse, to trust, to hope, and to endure whatever comes. *1 Corinthians 13:4-7*

## Intercessions

Blessed are you, Creator of heaven
    and earth,
  —you made the world and offer it
    life.

Remember us as we begin our work,,
  —that we work in harmony with
    others.

May we do what is useful for our
    brothers and sisters,
  —and together build a world that is
    pleasing to you.

To us and all whom we meet today,
  —give your joy and peace.

Our Father...

*(Morning Prayer, p. 32)*

# Wednesday Evening

Yahweh is my light and my salvation, whom need I fear? Yahweh is the fortress of my life, of whom should I be afraid?

One thing I ask of Yahweh, one thing I seek: to live in the house of Yahweh all the days of my life, to enjoy the sweetness of Yahweh and to consult him in his Temple.

Yahweh, hear my voice as I cry! Pity me! Answer me! My heart has said of you, 'Seek his face'. Yahweh, I do seek your face; do not hide your face from me.

*Psalm 27*

Glory to the Father...

## Reading

May the Lord be generous in increasing your love and make you love one

another and the whole human race as much as we love you. And may he so confirm your hearts in holiness that you may be blameless in the sight of our God and Father when our Lord Jesus Christ comes *with all his saints*.
*1 Thessalonians 3:12-13*

## Intercessions

Jesus, our Savior, from your pierced heart the church was born,
—by your holy Cross give us new life.

Jesus, our Savior, the centurion proclaimed you were God's Son,
—by your holy Cross increase our faith.

Jesus, our Savior, you called the good thief into paradise,
—by your holy Cross, call us.

Jesus, our Savior, you cured the sick and raised the dead,
—by your holy Cross, save us.

Our Father...

*(Evening Prayer, p. 33)*

# Thursday Morning

Acclaim Yahweh, all the earth, serve
 Yahweh gladly, come into his
 presence with songs of joy!

Know that he, Yahweh, is God, he
 made us and we belong to him,
 we are his people, the flock that
 he pastures.

Walk through his porticos giving
 thanks, enter his courts praising him,
 give thanks to him, bless his name!

Yes, Yahweh is good, his love is
 everlasting, his faithfulness endures
 from age to age.

*Psalm 100*

Glory to the Father...

## Reading

Finally: you should all agree among
yourselves and be sympathetic; love
the brothers, have compassion and be

self-effacing. Never pay back one wrong with another, or an angry word with another one; instead, pay back with a blessing. That is what you are called to do, so that you inherit a blessing yourself.

*1 Peter 3:8-9*

## Intercessions

Lord, our refuge and strength, listen to our praise at the beginning of this day,
—teach us to praise you without end.

In you we place our faith and hope,
—that our waiting might be rewarded.

You know our needs and come to our aid,
—without you we can do nothing.

Remember the poor and unfortunate,
—may this day not be a burden to them.

Our Father...

*(Morning Prayer, p. 32)*

# Thursday Evening

High praise, Yahweh, I give you, for you have helped me up, and not let my enemies gloat over me. Yahweh, my God, I cried to you for help, and you have healed me.

You have turned my mourning into dancing, you have stripped off my sackcloth and wrapped me in gladness; and now my heart, silent no longer, will play you music; Yahweh, my God, I will praise you for ever.

*Psalm 30*

So my soul sings praise to you unceasingly. O Lord my God, I will thank you forever.

Glory to the Father...

## Reading

This is a cause of great joy for you, even though you may for a short time have to bear being plagued by all sorts of trials; so that, when Jesus Christ is revealed, your faith will have been tested and proved like gold—only it is more precious than gold, which is corruptible even though it bears testing by fire—and then you will have praise and glory and honour. You did not see him, yet you love him; and still without seeing him, you are already filled with a joy so glorious that it cannot be described, because you believe; and you are sure of the end to which your faith looks forward, that is, the salvation of your souls.

*1 Peter 1:6-9*

## Intercessions

We praise you, God the Father, for the
    life you give us today,
  —blessed are you, O Lord.
We praise you for your Son who fills us
    with wisdom and knowledge,
  —blessed are you, O Lord.
We praise you, Father of mercies, for
    preserving us from temptation,
  —blessed are you, O Lord.
We praise you, God of kindness, for
    giving strength to the weak,
  —blessed are you, O Lord.
Our Father... *(Evening Prayer, p. 33)*

# Friday Morning

Have mercy on me, O God, in your goodness, in your great tenderness wipe away my faults; wash me clean of my guilt, purify me from my sin.

God, create a clean heart in me, put into me a new and constant spirit, do not banish me from your presence, do not deprive me of your holy spirit.

Be my saviour again, renew my joy, keep my spirit steady and willing; and I shall teach transgressors the way to you, and to you the sinners will return.

*Psalm 51*

Glory to the Father...

### Reading

Guard against foul talk; let your words be for the improvement of others, as occasion offers, and do good to your listeners, otherwise you will only be grieving the Holy Spirit of God who has marked you with his seal for you to be set free when the day comes. Never have grudges against others, or lose your temper, or raise your voice to anybody, or call each other names, or allow any sort of spitefulness. Be friends with one another, and kind, forgiving each other as readily as God forgave you in Christ.

*Ephesians 4:29-32*

## Intercessions

We give you thanks Lord, for you are rich in mercy,
—for the great love with which you have loved us.

You are acting always in the world by the power of your Spirit,
—making all things new.

Open our eyes today, and those of our brothers and sisters
—that we may see your wonders.

Our Father...

*(Morning Prayer, p. 32)*

# Friday Evening

I sing your praises, God my King, I bless your name for ever and ever, blessing you day after day, and praising your name for ever and ever.

He, Yahweh, is merciful, tenderhearted, slow to anger, very loving, and universally kind; Yahweh's tenderness embraces all his creatures.

Patiently all creatures look to you to feed them throughout the year; quick to satisy every need, you feed them all with a generous hand.

*Psalm 145*

Glory to the Father...

## Reading

Nothing therefore can come between us and the love of Christ, even if we are troubled or worried, or being persecuted, or lacking food or clothes, or being threatened or even attacked. As scripture promised: *For your sake we are being massacred daily, and reckoned as sheep for the slaughter.* These are the trials through which we triumph, by the power of him who loved us.

*Romans 8:35-37*

## Intercessions

Jesus, who died on the Cross for us,
> forgive the sins we have committed this day,
> —Lord, hear us! Lord, help us!

Jesus, conqueror of death, take our
> deceased brothers and sisters with you into paradise,
> —Lord, hear us! Lord, help us!

Jesus, born of Mary, give us a readiness
> like hers to welcome your word,
> —Lord, hear us! Lord, help us!

Our Father...

*(Evening Prayer, p. 33)*

## Saturday Morning

Praise Yahweh, all nations, extol him, all you peoples! For his love is strong, his faithfulness eternal.

*Psalm 117*

Praise the Lord, faraway space, glorify him, every home and family! For he has brought us to the beginning of this day, and he will see us to its end.

Praise the Lord, world of today, come with your blessings; come with your struggles.

Praise the Lord!

Glory to the Father...

### Reading

And may he who helps us when we refuse to give up, help you all to be tolerant with each other, following the example of Christ Jesus, so that united in mind and voice you may give glory to the God and Father of our Lord Jesus Christ. Accept one another, then, as Christ accepted you, for the glory of God.

*Romans 15:5-7*

## Intercessions

O God, you are our blessed light,
—awaken us this new day.

By the resurrection of your Son, you have enlightened the world,
—and given us new hope.

By your Spirit you gave wisdom to the disciples of your Son,
—send your Spirit upon us and make us faithful.

Light of the nations, shine on those who dwell in darkness,
—open their eyes to know you, the only true God.

Our Father...

*(Morning Prayer, p. 32)*

## Saturday Evening

From the depths I call to you, Yahweh,
 Lord, listen to my cry for help! Listen
 compassionately to my pleading!
*Psalm 130*

From my fears, failures and sins, I cry to
 you. Lord hear my voice.

From the depths of my heart I cry to
 you, from the darkness of myself.
 From life's shadow I cry to you.
 Lord, hear my voice.

For you are merciful, Lord, forgiving to
 us all. And so I wait, Lord, your
 mercy comes as sure as the dawn.

Glory to the Father...

### Reading

'The heart is more devious than any
other thing, perverse too: who can
pierce its secrets? I, Yahweh, search to

the heart, I probe the loins, to give each man what his conduct and his actions deserve.

*Jeremiah 17:9-10*

## Intercessions

O God, blessed through all ages, you guide us always with your light,
—we praise you through Jesus Christ.

O God, blessed through all ages, you nourish us with daily bread,
—we praise you through Jesus Christ.

O God, blessed through all ages, you strengthen us with your powerful grace,
—we praise you through Jesus Christ.

God of Glory, blessed through all ages, you glorify those who love you,
—we praise you through Jesus Christ.

Our Father...

*(Evening Prayer, p. 33)*

I come before you this evening, and in your presence remember now by name all whom I love (pause for silence).
May the spirit of evil have no power over me or over them, and may your holy angels keep us all in your peace. Amen.

# Prayer for Seasons of the Liturgical Year

# Advent

Father of our Lord Jesus Christ,
  ever faithful to your promises
  and ever close to your Church:
  the earth rejoices in hope of the
  Savior's coming
  and looks forward with longing
  to his return at the end of time.
Prepare my heart during this Advent
  Season.
Increase my longing for Christ my Savior
  and give me the strength
  to grow in love.

Jesus, my Lord,
  save me from my sins.
Come, protect me from all dangers
  and lead me to salvation.

Sanctify me in mind and body, Lord,
  keep me without sin until the coming
  of your Son.
Make me walk these days in holiness,
  Lord, and live an upright and
  devout life in this world.

Prepare a path in my heart
   for the coming of your Word
   and let his glory be revealed through
   my good works.

Bring low the mountains of my pride,
   Lord, and fill up the valleys
   of my weakness.

Keep me in the love of your Spirit,
   Lord, that I may receive the mercy
   of your Son who is to come.

I long for the grace of your coming,
   Lord, console me with the gift
   of your own divine life.

# Christmas

God of love
   the darkness that covered the earth
   has given way to the bright dawn
   of your Word made flesh.
Help me to walk in this light.
May I be faithful to your Word and
   bring your life to the waiting world.

At this time of your holy birth,
   Lord Jesus, I pray that my life
   may give glory to you.
Since your birth was here on earth,
   I hope you will someday
   give me my own birth in heaven.

You saved me by your birth, Lord Jesus
   help me to be faithful
   to the promises of my baptism.

Increase the hope of the weak, the poor
   and the aged,
   give relief to the oppressed and
   consolation to those who mourn.

You are the Prince of peace, Lord Jesus,
  grant the world that peace
  which the angels proclaimed.

Give me a heart
  that is upright and sincere
  so that I may listen to your word.

You shine on those who dwell in darkness,
  give me holiness, justice and peace.

You became our brother by being born
  of the Virgin Mary,
  teach me to love all
  as my brothers and sisters.

# Lent

Heavenly Father, I am called to walk by
  the light of Christ, your Son,
  and to trust in his wisdom.
During Lent, I submit my self to him
  more and more
  and am striving to believe in him
  with all my heart.
I enter on this path of repentance so
  that in dying to self
  I might rise to new life.


Lord Jesus, you spoke peace
  to a sinful world
  and brought mankind the gift of
  reconciliation by the suffering and
  death you endured.
I love you and joyfully bear the name
  'Christian'.
Teach me to follow your example.
Increase my faith, hope and charity
  so that I may struggle to turn hatred
  to love and conflict to peace.

Loving Redeemer through your passion,
   teach me self-denial,
   strengthen me against evil and
   adversity and so make me ready
   to celebrate your Resurrection.

Healer of body and soul,
   cure the sickness in my spirit
   so that I may grow in holiness
   through your constant care.

Forgive my sins
   against the unity of your family,
   make me love as you loved me.

Good Master, make me mindful of
   the dignity you gave me in Baptism,
   may I live for you at every moment.

Give me a perfect heart
   to receive your work, that
   I may bring forth fruit in patience.

Renew my eagerness to work with you
   in building a better world,
   so that my friends may hear your
   gospel of peace and justice.

# Easter

Heavenly Father and God of mercy,
　I believe that Jesus is alive and
　has become the Lord of life.
From the waters of Baptism you have
　raised me with him
　and renewed your gift of life within
　me.
Increase in my mind and heart the risen
　life I share with Christ
　and help me to grow in your wisdom
　and grace.


Lord Jesus, you appeared to your
　apostles after the resurrection and
　filled their hearts with joy when you
　said to them, "Peace be with you".
May the peace of your presence abide
　with me and make each day
　you give me the most beautiful day
　of my life.

Lord Jesus, you triumphed over death
　and destroyed the power of death in me,
　may I live only for you.

Risen Lord, you brought confusion on the guards at your tomb but joy to your disciples, grant me the fullness of joy as I serve you in spirit and truth.

You promised to be with your disciples, Lord, to the end of the world, stay with me today and remain with me always.

King of glory, center of my life, grant that when you come again, I may be one with you in glory.

Lord, remember me as in my own way I minister to your people, may my life be holy and an example to your people.

Lord Jesus, purify my heart with your truth and guide me in the way of holiness, so that I may always do what is pleasing in your sight.

## Pentecost

Father of light, from whom every good
  gift comes, send your Spirit into my
  life with the power of a mighty wind.
May he recall to my memory the words
  of Jesus and keep them in my heart.

Jesus, your Spirit renews the face of the
  earth and fills the whole universe,
May it renew the depth of my heart so
  that you may always find in my heart
  and on my lips a prayer pleasing to
  you.

Lord Jesus, when you were raised high
  upon the cross, streams of living water
  flowed from your pierced side, pour
  out on me your life-giving Spirit.

You promised to send the Holy Spirit
  to bear witness to yourself,
  renew your Spirit within me
  to make me your faithful witness.

You desire the whole world to be filled
  with your Spirit,
    help me to build a world of justice
  and peace.

You desire the unity of all Christians
  through one baptism in the Spirit,
  make all who believe one in heart and
  soul.

Lord Jesus, you gave your Spirit to the
  apostles with the power to forgive
  sins, destroy all sin in the world.

You promised the Holy Spirit to teach
  and remind your followers of all
  you have said, send me that Spirit
  to enlighten my mind in faith.

# Prayer for Our Parish

O God, you have made us the Church
of your dear Son.
Make our parish a family of one heart
and mind in love toward you.
Grant that our common life and work
may be an example to all about us.
Guide our pastor and his assistants
in their work.
Acknowledge the intercessions of
(Name of the parish patron)
our patron;
and keep us secure in your love.
Amen.

# Devotions Before and After Communion

# Prayers Before Communion

## Jesus, the Bread of Life

Father in heaven,
    you have made us for yourself;
    our hearts are restless
    until they rest in you.
Fulfill this longing through Jesus
    the bread of life,
    so that we may witness to Him
    who alone satisfies the hungers
    of the human family.
By the power of your spirit
    lead us to the heavenly table
    where we may feast on the vision of
    your glory for ever and ever. Amen.

## Prayer before Holy Communion

Come, O blessed Savior, and
 nourish my soul with heavenly Food,
 the Food which contains
 every sweetness and every delight.
Come, Bread of Angels,
 and satisfy the hunger of my soul.
Come, glowing Furnace of Charity,
 and enkindle in my heart
 the flame of divine love.
Come, Light of the World, and
 enlighten the darkness of my mind.
Come, King of Kings, and
 make me obedient to Your holy will.
Come, loving Savior, and
 make me meek and humble.
Come, Friend of the Sick, and
 heal the infirmities of my body and
 the weakness of my soul.
Come, Good Shepherd, my God and
 my All, and take me to Yourself.

## Prayer to the Virgin Mary

Mother of mercy and love,
   blessed Virgin Mary,
   I am poor and unworthy
   and I turn to you in confidence
   and love.
You stood by your Son
   as he hung dying on the cross.
Stand also by me, and by all
   who are offering Mass today here and
   throughout the entire Church.
Help us to offer a perfect and
   acceptable sacrifice in the sight
   of the holy and undivided Trinity,
   our most high God. Amen.

## Prayer of St. Thomas Aquinas

Almighty and ever-living God,
   I approach the sacrament of your
   only-begotten Son,
   our Lord Jesus Christ.
I come sick to the doctor of life,
   unclean to the fountain of mercy,
   blind to the radiance of eternal light,

and poor and needy to the Lord of
heaven and earth.
Lord, in your great generosity,
   heal my sickness,
   wash away my defilement,
   enlighten my blindness,
   enrich my poverty,
   and clothe my nakedness.
May I receive the bread of angels,
   the King of kings and Lord of lords,
   with humble reverence,
   with the purity and faith,
   the repentance and love,
   and the determined purpose that
   will help to bring me to salvation.
May I receive the sacrament
   of the Lord's body and blood,
   and its reality and power.
Kind God, may I receive the body
   of your only begotten Son,
   our Lord Jesus Christ,
   born from the womb
   of the Virgin Mary, and
   so be received into his mystical body
   and numbered among his members.
Loving Father,
   as on my earthly pilgrimage

I now receive your beloved Son
under the veil of a sacrament,
may I one day see him
face to face in glory,
who lives and reigns with you for ever.
Amen.


## Prayer of St. Ambrose

Lord Jesus Christ,
I approach your banquet table
  in fear and trembling,
  for I am a sinner,
  and dare not rely on my own worth
  but only on your goodness and mercy.
I am defiled by many sins in body and soul,
  and by my unguarded thoughts and words.
Gracious God of majesty and awe,
  I seek your protection,
  I look for your healing.
Poor troubled sinner that I am,
  I appeal to you, the fountain of all mercy.

I cannot bear your judgment,
    but I trust in your salvation.
Lord, I show my wounds to you
    and uncover my shame before you.
I know my sins are many and great,
    and they fill me with fear,
    but I hope in your mercies,
    for they cannot be numbered.
Lord Jesus Christ, eternal king,
    God and man,
    crucified for mankind,
    look upon me with mercy
    and hear my prayer,
    for I trust in you.
Have mercy on me,
    full of sorrow and sin,
    for the depth of your compassion
    never ends.
Praise to you, saving sacrifice,
    offered on the wood of the cross
    for me and for all mankind.
Praise to the noble and precious blood,
    flowing from the wounds
    of my crucified Lord Jesus Christ
    and washing away the sins
    of the whole world.
Remember, Lord, your creature,

whom you have redeemed
with your blood.
I repent my sins, and
I long to put right what I have done.
Merciful Father,
take away all my offenses and sins;
purify me in body and soul,
and make me worthy to taste
the holy of holies.
May your body and blood,
which I intend to receive,
although I am unworthy,
be for me the remission of my sins,
the washing away of my guilt,
the end of my evil thoughts,
and the rebirth of my better instincts.
May it incite me to do the works
pleasing to you and profitable
to my health in body and soul,
and be a firm defense against
the wiles of my enemies. Amen

# Prayers after Communion

## Prayer to the Virgin Mary

Mary, holy virgin mother,
  I have received your Son, Jesus Christ.
With love you became his mother,
  gave birth to him, nursed him,
  and helped him grow to manhood.
With love I return him to you,
  to hold once more,
  to love with all your heart, and
  to offer to the Holy Trinity
  as our supreme act of worship
  for your honor and for the good of
  all your pilgrim brothers and sisters.

Mother, ask God to forgive my sins and
  to help me serve him more faithfully.
Keep me true to Christ until death, and
  let me come to praise him with you
  for ever and ever. Amen.

## Prayer to our Redeemer

Jesus, may all that is you flow into me.
May your body and blood be my food
   and drink.
May your passion and death be my
   strength and life.
Jesus, with you by my side enough has
   been given.
May the shelter I seek be the shadow of
   your cross.
Let me not run from the love which you
   offer, but hold me safe
   from the forces of evil.
On each of my dyings shed your light
   and your love.
Keep calling to me until that day
   comes, when, with your saints,
   I may praise you for ever. Amen.


## The Anima Christi

Soul of Christ, sanctify me.
Body of Christ, save me.
Blood of Christ, inebriate me.
Water from the side of Christ, wash me.
Passion of Christ, strengthen me.

O good Jesus, hear me.
Within your wounds, hide me.
Permit me never to be separated from
 you.
From the malignant enemy, defend me.
In the hour of my death, call me
 and bid me to come to you,
 that with your Saints, I may praise you
 for ever and ever. Amen.

## Prayer to Jesus Christ Crucified

My good and dear Jesus,
I kneel before you
 asking you most earnestly
 to engrave upon my heart
 a deep and lively faith, hope, and charity,
 with true repentance for my sins,
 and a firm resolve to make amends.
As I reflect upon your five wounds,
 and dwell upon them with deep
 compassion and grief,
I recall, good Jesus, the words the
 prophet David spoke
 long ago concerning yourself:
 they have pierced my hands and feet,
 they have counted all my bones!

# Prayer of St. Thomas Aquinas

Lord, Father all-powerful
and ever-living God,
I thank you,
for even though I am a sinner,
your unprofitable servant,
not because of my worth but
in the kindness of your mercy,
you have fed me with the precious
body and blood of your Son,
our Lord Jesus Christ.
I pray that this holy communion
may not bring me
condemnation and punishment but
forgiveness and salvation.

May it be a helmet of faith
and a shield of good will.
May it purify me from evil ways
and put an end to my evil passions.
May it bring me charity and patience,
humility and obedience,
and growth in the power to do good.
May it be my strong defense against
all my enemies, visible and invisible,
and the perfect calming of all my evil
impulses, bodily and spiritual.

May it unite me more closely to you,
   the one true God,
   and lead me safely through death
   to everlasting happiness with you.

And I pray that you will lead me,
   a sinner, to the banquet where you,
   with your Son and Holy Spirit,
   are true and perfect light,
   total fulfillment, everlasting joy,
   gladness without end,
   and perfect happiness to your saints.
Grant this through Christ our Lord.
   Amen.


## Act of Thanksgiving

From the depths of my heart
   I thank You, Lord,
   for Your infinite kindness
   in coming to me.
How good You are to me!
With Your most holy Mother and all
   the angels, I praise Your mercy and
   generosity toward me.

I thank You for nourishing my soul
  with Your Sacred Body and
  Precious Blood.
I will try to show my gratitude to you
  in the Sacrament of Your love,
  by loving obedience
  to Your holy commandments,
  by fidelity to my duties,
  by kindness to my neighbor and
  by an earnest endeavor to become
  more like You in my daily conduct.

Grant that I may spend the hours
  of the day gladly working with You
  according to Your will.

May I not lose my enthusiasm
  in serving you.
May my conversations
  be occasions of charity.
May I be patient with myself
  and those around me
  in the day's disappointments.
May I be mindful of others
  rather than myself in moments
  of fatigue and illness.

May I be generous and faithful
   so that when this day is over
   I may feel that life
   is really meaningful and peaceful
   for it has been spent
   in your loving company. Amen.


## Prayer of Self-Dedication to Jesus Christ

Lord Jesus Christ
   take all my freedom,
   my memory, my understanding, and
   my will.
All that I have and cherish
   you have given me.
I surrender it all to be guided by your
   will.
Your grace and your love
   are wealth enough for me.
Give me these, Lord Jesus,
   and I ask for nothing more.

# Prayer for Love of God

O great Lord of heaven and earth,
infinite good and majesty,
you who have loved men so tenderly,
how is it that you are despised by
so many human beings?
You have loved me
in a special manner
and have bestowed
many wonderful graces on me.
Yet I, too, have despised you
by every sin through which
I have turned against your law.
I resolve this day to love you
with my whole heart and to love
nothing unless it can be loved in you.
Grant me this gift of love:
a fervent love that will make me reject
the appeal of sinful creatures;
a strong love that will make me
conquer all difficulties to please you;
a persevering love that will never be
dissolved. Amen.

# Sacrament of Reconciliation

# The Sacrament of Reconciliation

God our Father has reconciled us to Himself by the life, death and resurrection of Jesus. We apply this forgiveness to ourselves when we come as penitents to the Lord in the Sacrament of Reconciliation.

Each penitent remembers that the Father has called him or her to a life of holiness in Jesus the Lord. The individual penitent then first seeks the light of the Holy Spirit upon his or her life to surface areas of infidelity in responding to that call.

# Prayer of Preparation and Examination of Conscience

Holy Spirit
  you came down upon the Apostles
  to enlighten their minds and
  strengthen their ministry.
Come down upon me
  at this important moment.
Help me to see my life
  in the light of Jesus Christ.
Renew my love as I am reconciled to God
  and his people.

*Examine your life in the light of God's word.*

I. **The Lord says: "You shall love the Lord your God with your whole heart."**

    1. Is my heart set on God, so that I really love him above all things and am faithful to his commandments, as a son loves his father? Or am I more concerned about the things of this world? Have I a right intention in what I do?

2. God spoke to us in his Son. Is my faith in God firm and secure? Am I wholehearted in accepting the Church's teaching? Have I been careful to grow in my understanding of the faith, to hear God's word, to listen to instructions on the faith, to avoid dangers to faith? Have I been always strong and fearless in professing my faith in God and the Church? Have I been willing to be known as a Christian in private and public life?

3. Have I prayed morning and evening? When I pray, do I really raise my mind and heart to God or is it a matter of words only? Do I offer God my difficulties, my joys, and my sorrows? Do I turn to God in time of temptation?

4. Have I love and reverence for God's name? Have I offended him in blasphemy, swearing falsely, or taking his name in vain? Have I shown disrespect for the Blessed Virgin Mary and the saints?

5. Do I keep Sundays and feast days holy by taking a full part, with attention and devotion, in the liturgy, and especially in the Mass? Have I fulfilled the precept of annual confession and of communion during the Easter season?

6. Are there false gods that I worship by giving them greater attention and deeper trust than I give to God: money, superstition, spiritism, or other occult practices?

II. **The Lord says: "Love one another as I have loved you."**

1. Have I a genuine love for my neighbors? Or do I use them for my own ends, or do to them what I would not want done to myself? Have I given grave scandal by my words or actions?

2. In my family life, have I contributed to the well-being and happiness of the rest of the family by patience and genuine love? Have I been obedient to parents, showing

them proper respect and giving them help in their spiritual and material needs? Have I been careful to give a Christian upbringing to my children, and to help them by good example and by exercising authority as a parent? Have I been faithful to my husband (wife) in my heart and in my relations with others?

3. Do I share my possessions with the less fortunate? Do I do my best to help the victims of oppression, misfortune, and poverty? Or do I look down on my neighbor, especially the poor, the sick, the elderly, strangers, and people of other races?

4. Does my life reflect the mission I received in confirmation? Do I share in the apostolic and charitable works of the Church and in the life of my parish? Have I helped to meet the needs of the Church and of the world and prayed for them: for unity in the Church, for the spread of the Gospel among the nations, for peace and justice, etc?

5. Am I concerned for the good and prosperity of the human community in which I live, or do I spend my life caring only for myself? Do I share to the best of my ability in the work of promoting justice, morality, harmony, and love in human relations? Have I done my duty as a citizen? Have I paid my taxes?

6. In my work or profession am I just, hard-working, honest, serving society out of love for others? Have I paid a fair wage to my employees? Have I been faithful to my promises and contracts?

7. Have I obeyed legitimate authority and given it due respect?

8. If I am in a position of responsibility or authority, do I use this for my own advantage or for the good of others, in a spirit of service?

9. Have I been truthful and fair, or have I injured others by deceit, calumny, detraction, rash judgment, or violation of a secret?

10. Have I done violence to others by damage to life or limb, reputation, honor, or material possessions? Have I involved them in loss? Have I been responsible for advising an abortion or procuring one? Have I kept up hatred for others? Am I estranged from others through quarrels, enmity, insults, anger? Have I been guilty of refusing to testify to the innocence of another because of selfishness?

11. Have I stolen the property of others? Have I desired it unjustly and inordinately? Have I damaged it? Have I made restitution of other people's property and made good their loss?

12. If I have been injured, have I been ready to make peace for the love of Christ and to forgive, or do I harbor hatred and the desire for revenge?

III. **Christ our Lord says: "Be perfect as your Father is perfect."**

1. Where is my life really leading me? Is the hope of eternal life my inspiration? Have I tried to grow in the life of the Spirit through prayer, reading the word of God and meditating on it, receiving the sacraments, self-denial? Have I been anxious to control my vices, my bad inclinations and passions, e.g., envy, love of food and drink? Have I been proud and boastful, thinking myself better in the sight of God and despising others as less important than myself? Have I imposed my own will on others, without respecting their freedom and rights?

2. What use have I made of time, of health and strength, of the gifts God has given me to be used like the talents in the Gospel? Do I use them to become more perfect every day? Or have I been lazy and too much given to leisure?

3. Have I been patient in accepting the sorrows and disappointments of life? How have I performed mortification so as to "fill up what is wanting to the sufferings of Christ"? Have I kept the precept of fasting and abstinence?

4. Have I kept my senses and my whole body pure and chaste as a temple of the Holy Spirit consecrated for resurrection and glory, and as a sign of God's faithful love for men and women, a sign that is seen most perfectly in the sacrament of matrimony? Have I dishonored my body by fornication, impurity, unworthy conversation or thoughts, evil desires, or actions? Have I given in to sensuality? Have I indulged in reading, conversation, shows, and entertainments that offend against Christian and human decency? Have I encouraged others to sin by my own failure to maintain these standards? Have I been faithful to the moral law in my married life?

5. Have I gone against my conscience out of fear or hypocrisy?

6. Have I always tried to act in the true freedom of the sons of God according to the law of the Spirit, or am I the slave of forces within me?

## Prayer of the Penitent and Absolution

My God,
I am sorry for my sins with all my heart.
In choosing to do wrong
   and failing to do good,
     I have sinned against you
     whom I should love above all things.
I firmly intend, with your help,
   to do penance,
   to sin no more,
   and to avoid whatever leads me to sin.
Our Savior Jesus Christ
   suffered and died for us.
In his name, my God, have mercy.

## Absolution

If the penitent is not kneeling, he or she bows his or her head as the priest extends his hands (or at least extends his right hand).

God, the Father of mercies,
 through the death and resurrection
 of his Son
 has reconciled the world to himself
 and sent the Holy Spirit among us
 for the forgiveness of sins;
 through the ministry of the Church
 may God give you pardon and peace,
 and I absolve you from your sins
 in the name of the Father,
 and of the Son,
 and of the Holy Spirit.

The penitent answers: Amen.

# Dismissal

Priest: Give thanks to the Lord, for he is good.

Penitent: His mercy endures for ever.

Then the penitent is dismissed by the priest.

Father,
   we are sinners,
   like the prodigal in the story;
   jealous, too, like the older brother.
But you accept us just as we are,
   and always welcome us home,
   with open arms.
Help us to accept one another
   and forgive one another
   with the same easiness with which
   you forgive us.
We pray for it, in the name of Jesus.
   Amen.

# Prayer for Goodness

O Holy Spirit of God,
  take me as your disciple.
  Guide me, illuminate me, sanctify me.
  Bind my hands
  that they may do no evil;
  cover my eyes
  that they may see it no more;
  sanctify my heart
  that evil may not dwell within me.
  Be my guide;
  wherever you lead me, I will go;
  whatever you forbid me,
  I will renounce;
  and whatever you command me
  in your strength,
  I will do.
  Lead me then to the fullness
  of your truth. Amen.

# Devotions to our Lord in the Blessed Sacrament

# Act of Trust

We can never make an end of our
  gratitude to thee, who never ceasest
  to cherish us with thy mercy.
Who can sufficiently praise the works
  of thy power, thou whose divine
  presence no human eye can see,
  whose greatness no words can tell?
Let it be sufficient, then, that
  we are able to love thee as our Father,
  reverence thee as our Ruler,
  acknowledge thee as our Creator,
  welcome thee as our Redeemer.
So as most gentle Ruler and Guide,
  lead us on that narrow path that
  thou wouldst have us ascend to the
  attainment of our lasting happiness.
  *(Gothic Missal, seventh century)*

# Act of Humility

Devoutly kneeling before thy Majesty,
  we earnestly pray that,
  since thou dost see the limits
  of our human weakness,
  thou wouldst not in anger blame us
  for our disobedience, but
  with thy boundless pity cleanse us,
  teach us and comfort us;
  and since if thou dost not help us,
  we cannot do what is well-pleasing
  in thy sight, let thy grace come to
  help us, that we may live to our own
  well-being, ever friends with thee.

*(Eleventh-century Missal)*

# Prayers for Others

O Lord God of strength, who are
true charity, unshaken tranquillity
and hope unfailing:
do thou, O Lord our God,
give to thy servants here present
in the sight of thy Majesty, the gifts
of charity, kindness, calmness and
lasting peace, that we may all in
purity of heart and goodness of soul
have peace with each other.
*(Liturgy of St. John)*

Be mindful, O Lord, of all those
who have asked us to remember them
in the prayers and petitions
we now make in thy sight.
O Lord our God,
be mindful of those whose memory
is always with us, and those who are
especially in our thoughts at this
moment and in our present prayer.
Bring them the grace of a strong and
lasting defense against
all that may harm them.
*(Coptic Liturgy)*

# Prayers for the Love of God

A man will have a great and long
 struggle with himself, before he fully
 learns to master self and to turn
 his whole affection towards God.
When a man relies on himself,
 he easily turns aside
 to human consolations.
But a true lover of Christ, and
 a diligent pursuer of virtue,
 does not fall back upon consolations,
 nor seek such sensible sweetnesses;
 he prefers hard trials and would wish
 to undergo severe labors for Christ.
*(Imitation of Christ)*


O my Lord Jesus, let me never
 for an instant forget
 that thou hast established
 on earth a kingdom of thy own;
 that the Church is thy work,
 thy establishment, thy instrument;
 that we are under thy rule;
 that where the Church speaks,
 thou dost speak.

Let not familiarity with this wonderful
truth lead me to be insensible to it.
*(John Henry Newman)*

O Christ our Lord, perfect lover of
mankind, grant, we beseech thee,
that there may ever abide in us,
knowledge, intelligence,
understanding and wisdom.
So may we see ever deeper and deeper,
and understand and appreciate the
lesson of thy holiness, which is open
before us in thy sight.
As thou didst so enrich Paul, making
him worthy of such great graces,
make us also, we beseech thee,
O Author of life, to imitate him
and follow closely in his footsteps.
*(Missa Ethiopum, tenth century)*

# Act of Spiritual Communion

Jesus, my Savior and my God!
I am not worthy to be before you,
   for I am a poor sinner;
   yet I approach you with confidence,
   for you have said, "Come to me,
   all you that labor and are heavy-laden,
   and I will refresh you."
You will not despise a contrite and
   humble heart.
I am truly sorry for my sins,
   because by them I have offended you,
   who are infinitely good.
Whatever may have been my foolish
   transgressions in the past, I love you
   now above all things,
   and with all my heart.

Come, my Lord, my God, and my all!
Come to me, and let me never again
   be separated from you by sin.
Teach me your blessed ways;
   help me with your grace to imitate
   your example; to practice meekness,
   humility, charity, and
   all the virtues of your Sacred Heart.

My divine Master, my desire is
   to do your will and to love you more
   and more; help me that I may be
   faithful to the end in your service.
Bless me in life and in death, that
   I may praise you forever in heaven.
   Amen.

## Eucharistic Offering

O Lord, to whom belongs all
   that is in heaven and earth,
   I desire to consecrate myself totally
   to you and to be yours forevermore.
I offer myself to you today, O Lord,
   in singleness of heart,
   to serve and obey you always, and
   I offer you without ceasing a sacrifice
   of praise and thanksgiving.
Receive me, O my Savior, in union
   with the holy oblation of your
   precious blood which I offer unto you

this day, in the presence of angels,
that this sacrifice may avail unto my
salvation and that of the entire world.
*Imitation of Christ, IV,9*

## Closing Prayer to the Blessed Sacrament

As my time of adoration closes,
 Lord Jesus,
 I renew my faith and trust in You.
I am refreshed after these moments
 with You, and I count myself
 among a privileged number,
 who are blessed to share
 Your sacramental presence.

I am resolved to go forth again to my
 duties and my concerns with a renewed
 spirit of perseverance and good will.
In my daily life I will try to love
 and serve God, our Father,
 and love my neighbor.
I will try to be a true disciple.
Help me, Jesus, in this resolution.

Bless me, Lord, before I go.
And bless not me alone
  but all my friends,
  especially the sick and the dying.
Bless our homes and
  all the children there.
Bless all our lives and
  the hour of our death.

Grant rest to the souls of the faithful
  departed and bring them into the
  light of Your divine glory.
May we who have worshiped You and
  been blessed by You here on earth,
  come to behold the radiant glory of
  Your unveiled countenance in
  heaven for ever and ever. Amen.

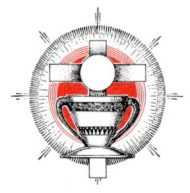

# Benediction

# Benediction of the Blessed Sacrament

Benediction of the Blessed Sacrament is intended to acknowledge Christ's marvelous presence in the sacrament. It invites us to a spiritual union with him that culminates in sacramental Communion. During the exposition there are readings, hymns and prayers to direct our attention to the worship of Christ the Lord.

## Readings:

### A. A reading from the Letter of Paul to the Philippians.

Though he was in the form of God
Jesus did not deem equality with God
something to be grasped at.

Rather, he emptied himself
and took the form of a slave,
being born in the likeness of men.

He was known to be of human estate,
and it was thus that he humbled
himself, obediently accepting even
death, death on a cross!

Because of this,
God highly exalted him
and bestowed on him the name
above every other name,
so that at Jesus' name
every knee must bend
in the heavens, on the earth,
and under the earth,
and every tongue proclaim
to the glory of God the Father:

JESUS CHRIST IS LORD!

B. A reading from the Gospel of John.

When the people saw that neither Jesus nor his disciples were there, they got into their boats and crossed to Capernaum to look for Jesus. When they found him on the other side, they said to him, 'Rabbi, when did you come here?' Jesus answered:

'I tell you most solemnly,
you are not looking for me
because you have seen the signs
and because you had all the bread
you wanted to eat.
Do not work for food that cannot last,
but work for food that endures to eternal life,
the kind of food the Son of Man is offering you,
for on him the Father, God himself,
has set his seal.'

Then they said to him, 'What must we do if we are to do the works that God wants?' Jesus gave them this answer, 'This is working for God: you must believe in the one he has sent'. So they said, 'What sign will you give to show us that we should believe in you? What work will you do? Our fathers had manna to eat in the desert; as scripture says: He gave them bread from heaven to eat.'

Jesus answered:

> 'I tell you most solemnly,
> It was not Moses who gave you
> bread from heaven, it is my Father
> who gives you the bread from
> heaven, the true bread;
> for the bread of God
> is that which comes down from
> heaven and gives life to the world'.

'Sir,' they said 'give us that bread always.' Jesus answered:

> 'I am the bread of life.
> He who comes to me will never be
> hungry; he who believes in me will
> never thirst.'

## Hymn:

> Down in adoration falling,
> Lo! the sacred host we hail;
> Lo! o'er ancient forms departing,
> Newer rites of grace prevail;
> Faith for all defects supplying,
> Where the feeble senses fail.

To the everlasting Father
And the Son who reigns on high,
With the Holy Ghost proceeding
Forth from each eternally,
Be salvation, honor, blessing,
Might and endless majesty. Amen.

V. You send them bread from heaven.
(Alleluia.)

R. Having in itself every delight.
(Alleluia.)

Let us pray.

O God, who under this wonderful sacrament has left us a memorial of your passion: grant, we beseech you, so to reverence the sacred mysteries of your body and blood, that we may ever feel within ourselves the fruit of your redemption. Who lives and reigns forever and ever. Amen.

**Prayers:**

Lord our God,
  in this great sacrament
  we come into the presence of
  Jesus Christ, your Son,
  born of the Virgin Mary
  and crucified for our salvation.
May we who declare our faith in this
  fountain of love and mercy
  drink from it the water of
  everlasting life.
We ask this through Christ our Lord.

Lord our God,
  may we always give due honor to
  the sacramental presence of the Lamb
  who was slain for us.
May our faith be rewarded
  by the vision of his glory,
  who lives and reigns for ever and ever.

Lord our God,
  you have given us the true bread
  from heaven.
In the strength of this food
  may we live always by your life
  and rise in glory on the last day.
We ask this through Christ our Lord.

# The Divine Praises

Blessed be God.
Blessed be his holy name.
Blessed be Jesus Christ, true God and true man.
Blessed be the name of Jesus.
Blessed be his most sacred heart.
Blessed be his most precious blood.
Blessed be Jesus in the most holy sacrament of the altar.
Blessed be the Holy Spirit, the Paraclete.
Blessed be the great mother of God, Mary most holy.
Blessed be her holy and immaculate conception.
Blessed be her glorious assumption.
Blessed be the name of Mary, virgin and mother.
Blessed be Saint Joseph, her most chaste spouse.
Blessed be God in his angels and in his saints.

# Devotions to the Sacred Heart of Jesus

# Devotions to the Sacred Heart of Jesus

*St. Margaret Mary Alacoque was born in France in 1647 and died in 1690. Our Lord appeared to St. Margaret Mary several times during her life as a nun in the Visitation Order. In 1675, the great revelation was made to St. Margaret Mary that she, along with Father de la Colombiere, S.J., was to be the chief instrument for instituting the Feast of the Sacred Heart and for spreading devotion to the Sacred Heart throughout the world.*

## The Great Promise of the First Friday

All who receive Holy Communion on nine consecutive First Fridays have been blessed by Our Lord with the grace of a most wonderful promise. We should listen carefully. It is our Saviour, Himself, who speaks to us through St. Margaret Mary:

"I promise you in the unfathomable mercy of My heart that My omnipotent love will procure the grace of final penitence for all those who communicate on nine successive First Fridays of the month; they will not die in My disfavor, or without having received their sacraments, since My divine heart will be their sure refuge in the last moments of their life."

Our Lord also told St. Margaret Mary of the following additional blessings:

1. I will give them all the graces necessary for their state of life.

2. I will establish peace in their families.

3. I will comfort them in all their afflictions.

4. I will be their secure refuge during life, and above all in death.

5. I will bestow a special blessing upon all their undertakings.

6. Sinners shall find in My heart the source and infinite ocean of mercy.

7. Tepid souls shall grow fervent.

8. Fervent souls shall quickly mount to high perfection.

9. I will bless every place where a picture of My heart shall be exposed and honored.

10. I will give to priests the gift of touching the most hardened hearts.

11. Those who shall promote this devotion shall have their names written in My heart—never to be blotted out.

# Act of Reparation to the Sacred Heart of Jesus

O sweet Jesus, whose overflowing charity for men is requited by so much forgetfulness, negligence and contempt, behold us prostrate before You eager to repair by a special act of homage the cruel indifference and injuries to which Your loving heart is everywhere subject.

Mindful alas! that we ourselves have had a share in such great indignities, which we now deplore from the depth of our hearts, we humbly ask Your pardon and declare our readiness to atone by voluntary expiation not only for our own personal offenses, but also for the sins of those, who, straying far from the path of salvation, refuse in their obstinate infidelity to follow You, their shepherd and leader, or, renouncing the vows of their baptism, have cast off the sweet yoke of Your law.

We are now resolved to expiate each

and every deplorable outrage committed against You, we are determined to make amends for the manifold offenses against Christian modesty in unbecoming dress and behavior, for all the foul seductions laid to ensnare the feet of the innocent, for the frequent violation of Sundays and holidays, and the shocking blasphemies uttered against You and Your saints.

We wish also to make amends for the insults to which Your vicar on earth and Your priests are subjected, for the profanation, by conscious neglect or terrible acts of sacrilege, of the very sacrament of Your divine love; and lastly for the public crimes of nations who resist the rights and the teaching authority of the Church which You have founded.

Would, O divine Jesus, we were able to wash away such abominations with our blood! We now offer in reparation for these violations of Your divine honor, the satisfaction You did once make to Your eternal Father on the Cross and which You continue to renew daily before us; we offer it in union with the acts of atonement of Your virgin mother and all the saints and of the pious faithful on earth; and we sincerely promise to make recompense as far as we can with the help of Your grace, for all neglect of Your great love and for the sins we and others have committed in the past.

Henceforth we will live a life of unwavering faith, of purity of conduct, of perfect observance of the precepts of the Gospel and especially that of charity.

We promise to the best of our power to prevent others from offending You and to bring as many as possible to follow You.

O loving Jesus, through the intercession of the Blessed Virgin Mary, our model in reparation, deign to receive the voluntary offering we make of this act of expiation; and by the crowning gift of perseverance keep us faithful unto death in our duty and the allegiance we owe to You, so that we may all one day come to that happy home, where You with the Father and the Holy Spirit live and reign, God, world without end. Amen.

# Act of Consecration of the Human Race to the Sacred Heart

Most sweet Jesus, Redeemer of the human race, look down upon us humbly prostrate before You. We are Yours, and Yours we wish to be; but to be more surely united with You, behold each one of us freely consecrates himself today to Your Most Sacred Heart. Many indeed have never known You; many too, despising Your precepts, have rejected You. Have mercy on them all, most merciful Jesus, and draw them to Your Sacred Heart. Be King, O Lord, not only of the faithful who have never forsaken You, but also of the prodigal children who have abandoned You; grant that they may quickly return to their Father's house lest they die of wretchedness and hunger. Be King of those who are deceived by erroneous opinions, or whom discord holds aloof, and call them back to the harbor of truth and unity of faith, so that soon there may be but one flock and one shepherd. Grant, O Lord, to Your Church assurance of freedom and immunity from harm; give peace and order to all nations, and make the earth resound from pole to pole with one cry: "Praise to the Divine Heart that wrought our salvation; to it be glory and honor forever." Amen.

*The Litany of the Sacred Heart of Jesus can be found on page* 135, *and the Novena in honor of the Sacred Heart of Jesus can be found on page* 170.

# Litanies

# Litanies

A litany, by definition, is a prayer of brief invocations said alternately, and with responses. There are many litanies which have proven to be popular with the faithful, but only five of them have been approved for public devotion. They are:

1. Litany of the Sacred Heart
2. Litany of the Most Holy Name of Jesus
3. Litany of the Blessed Virgin Mary
4. Litany of St. Joseph
5. Litany of the Saints

# Litany of the Sacred Heart of Jesus

Lord, have mercy.
Christ, have mercy.
Lord, have mercy. Christ, hear us.
Christ, graciously hear us.
God the Father of heaven,
—Have mercy on us.
God the Son, Redeemer of the world,
*(After each invocation, respond with, "Have mercy on us.")*
God the Holy Spirit,
Holy Trinity, one God,
Heart of Jesus, Son of the eternal Father,
Heart of Jesus, formed by the Holy Spirit in the womb of the Virgin Mary,
Heart of Jesus, united with God's eternal Word,
Heart of Jesus, of limitless majesty,
Heart of Jesus, temple of God among us,
Heart of Jesus, shrine of the Most High,
Heart of Jesus, house of God and gate of heaven,
Heart of Jesus, glowing with love for us,

Heart of Jesus, overflowing with goodness and love,
Heart of Jesus, full of kindness and love,
Heart of Jesus, fountain of all holiness,
Heart of Jesus, worthy of all praise,
Heart of Jesus, king and center of all hearts,
Heart of Jesus, treasure-house of wisdom and knowledge,
Heart of Jesus, tabernacle of God's fullness,
Heart of Jesus, in whom the Father is well pleased,
Heart of Jesus, of whose fullness we have all received,
Heart of Jesus, desire of the everlasting hills,
Heart of Jesus, patient and full of mercy,
Heart of Jesus, generous to all who turn to you,
Heart of Jesus, source of life and holiness,
Heart of Jesus, atonement for our sins,
Heart of Jesus, overwhelmed with reproaches,
Heart of Jesus, bruised for our sins,
Heart of Jesus, obedient all the way to death,

Heart of Jesus, pierced with a lance,
Heart of Jesus, source of all consolation,
Heart of Jesus, our life and resurrection,
Heart of Jesus, our peace and reconciliation,
Heart of Jesus, sacrifice for sin,
Heart of Jesus, salvation of all who trust in you,
Heart of Jesus, hope of all who die in you,
Heart of Jesus, delight of all the saints,

Lamb of God, you take away the sins of the world, —Spare us, O Lord.

Lamb of God, you take away the sins of the world, —Graciously hear us, O Lord.

Lamb of God, you take away the sins of the world, —Have mercy on us.

Jesus, gentle and humble of heart,
—Touch our hearts and make them like your own.

Let us pray.

Father, rejoice in the gifts of love
   we have received from the heart of Jesus your Son.
Open our hearts to share his life
   and continue to bless us with his love.
We ask this through Christ our Lord.
   Amen.

# Litany of the Most Holy Name of Jesus

Lord, have mercy.
Christ, have mercy.
Lord, have mercy.
Christ, hear us.
Christ, graciously hear us.
God, the Father of heaven,
                —Have mercy on us.
God, the Son, Redeemer of the world,
*(After each invocation, respond with, "Have mercy on us.")*
God the Holy Spirit,
Holy Trinity, one God,
Jesus, Son of the living God,
Jesus, splendor of the Father,
Jesus, brightness of eternal light,
Jesus, king of glory,
Jesus, sun of justice,
Jesus, Son of the Virgin Mary,
Jesus, worthy of all our love,
Jesus, our wonderful delight,
Jesus, mighty God,
Jesus, Father of the world to come,

Jesus, messenger of great counsel,
Jesus, most powerful,
Jesus, most patient,
Jesus, most obedient,
Jesus, gentle and humble of heart,
Jesus, lover of chastity,
Jesus, lover of the human family,
Jesus, God of peace,
Jesus, author of life,
Jesus, pattern of all virtues,
Jesus, zealous lover of souls,
Jesus, our God,
Jesus, our refuge,
Jesus, father of the poor,
Jesus, treasure of the faithful,
Jesus, good shepherd,
Jesus, true light,
Jesus, eternal wisdom,
Jesus, unbounded goodness,
Jesus, our way and our life,
Jesus, joy of angels,
Jesus, king of patriarchs,
Jesus, master of apostles,
Jesus, teacher of evangelists,
Jesus, strength of martyrs,
Jesus, light of confessors,
Jesus, purity of virgins,

Jesus, crown of all the saints,

Be merciful, —Jesus, spare us.
Be merciful, —Jesus, hear and heed us.
From all evil, —Jesus, deliver us.
From all sin, *(After each invocation, respond with, "Jesus, deliver us.")*
From the anger of a righteous God,
From the snares of the devil,
From the spirit of uncleanness,
From everlasting death,
From neglect of your inspirations,
By the mystery of your holy incarnation,
By your birth in the stable of Bethlehem,
By your affectionate and obedient childhood,
By your divine and exemplary life,
By your labors on our behalf,
By your agony and passion,
By your cross and desolation,
By your death and burial,
By your glorious resurrection and wonderful ascension,
By the institution of the holy Eucharist,
By your joys and by your glory,

Lamb of God, you take away the sins of
   the world,         —Spare us, O Jesus.

Lamb of God, you take away the sins of
   the world, —Jesus, hear and heed us.

Lamb of God, you take away the sins of
   the world,
         —Have mercy on us, O Jesus.

Our help is in the Name of the Lord,
   —The maker of heaven and earth.

Let us pray.

O God, our loving Father,
   you appointed your Son to be the
   Savior of the human race and
   commanded that he should be called
   Jesus.
Look with favor on us, and
   grant that our respect
   for his holy Name on earth may lead
   to our vision of him in heaven.
We ask this through Jesus our Lord.
   Amen.

# Litany of the Blessed Virgin Mary

Lord, have mercy.
Christ, have mercy.
Lord, have mercy.
Christ, hear us.
Christ, graciously hear us.
God, the Father of heaven, have mercy on us.
God, the Son, Redeemer of the world, have mercy on us.
God, the Holy Spirit, have mercy on us.
Holy Trinity, one God, have mercy on us.
Holy Mary,

—Pray for us.

Holy Mother of God, *(after each invocation, respond with, "Pray for us.")*

Holy Virgin of virgins,
Mother of Christ,
Mother, full of grace,
Mother most pure,
Mother most chaste,
Immaculate Mother,
Sinless Mother,
Lovable Mother,

Model of Mothers,
Mother of good counsel,
Mother of our Maker,
Mother of our Savior,
Wisest of virgins,
Holiest of virgins,
Noblest of virgins,
Virgin, powerful in the sight of God,
Virgin, merciful to us sinners,
Virgin, faithful to all God asks of you,
Mirror of holiness,
Seat of wisdom,
Cause of our joy,
Shrine of the Spirit,
Honor of your people,
Devoted handmaid of the Lord,
Mystical rose,
Tower of David,
Tower of ivory,
House of gold,
Ark of the covenant,
Gate of heaven,
Star of hope,
Health of the sick,
Refuge of sinners,
Comfort of the afflicted,
Help of Christians,

Queen of angels,
Queen of patriarchs,
Queen of prophets,
Queen of apostles,
Queen of martyrs,
Queen of confessors,
Queen of virgins,
Queen of all saints,
Queen conceived in holiness,
Queen raised up to glory,
Queen of the rosary,
Queen of peace,

Lamb of God, you take away the sins of the world, —Spare us, O Lord.

Lamb of God, you take away the sins of the world,
—Graciously hear us, O Lord.

Lamb of God, you take away the sins of the world, —Have mercy on us.

Pray for us, O holy Mother of God,
—That we may be made worthy of the promises of Christ.

Let us pray.

Lord God,
   give to your people the joy of
   continual health in mind and body.
With the prayers of the Virgin Mary
   to help us, guide us through
   the sorrows of this life to
   eternal happiness in the life to come.
We ask this through Christ our Lord.
   Amen.

# Litany of St. Joseph

Lord, have mercy.
Christ, have mercy.
Lord, have mercy.
Christ, hear us.
Christ, graciously hear us.
God, the Father of heaven, have mercy on us.
God, the son, Redeemer of the world, have mercy on us.
God the Holy Spirit, have mercy on us.
Holy Trinity, one God, have mercy on us.
Holy Mary, –Pray for us.
St. Joseph, *(After each invocation, respond with, "Pray for us.")*
Renowned descendent of David,
Light of patriarchs,
Husband of the Mother of God,
Chaste guardian of the Virgin,
Foster-father of the Son of God,
Watchful defender of Christ,
Head of the holy family,

Joseph, most just,
Joseph, most pure,
Joseph, most prudent,
Joseph, most valiant,
Joseph, most obedient,
Joseph, most faithful,
Mirror of patience,
Lover of poverty,
Model of artisans,
Glory of domestic life,
Guardian of virgins,
Mainstay of families,
Consolation of those in trouble,
Hope of the sick,
Patron of the dying,
Protector of holy Church.

Lamb of God, you take away the sins of the world,    —Spare us, O Lord.

Lamb of God, you take away the sins of the world,
—Graciously hear us, O Lord.

Lamb of God, you take away the sins of the world,    —Have mercy on us.

He made him lord of his household,

—And ruler over all his possessions.

Let us pray.

God,
    in your infinite wisdom and love
    you chose Joseph to be the husband
    of Mary, the mother of your Son.
May we have the help of his prayers
    in heaven and
    enjoy his protection on earth.
We ask this through Christ our Lord.
    Amen.

# Litany of the Saints

Lord, have mercy.
Christ, have mercy.
Lord, have mercy.
Christ, hear us.
Christ, graciously hear us.
God, the Father of heaven, have mercy on us.
God, the Son, Redeemer of the world, have mercy on us.
God the Holy Spirit, have mercy on us.
Holy Trinity, one God, have mercy on us.
Holy Mary,

—Pray for us.

Mother of God, *(After each invocation, respond with, "Pray for us.")*
Most honored of all virgins,
Michael, Gabriel and Raphael,
Angels of God,
Abraham, Moses and Elijah,
Saint John the Baptist,
Saint Joseph,
Holy patriarchs and prophets,

Saint Peter and Saint Paul,
Saint Andrew,
Saint John and Saint James,
Saint Thomas,
Saint Matthew,
All holy Apostles,
Saint Luke,
Saint Mark,
Saint Barnabas,
Saint Mary Magdalene,
All disciples of the Lord,
Saint Stephen,
Saint Ignatius,
Saint Polycarp,
Saint Justin,
Saint Lawrence,
Saint Cyprian,
Saint Boniface,
Saint Stanislaus,
Saint Thomas Becket,
Saint John Fisher and Saint Thomas More,
Saint Paul Miki,
Saint Isaac Jogues and Saint John de Brebeuf,
Saint Peter Chanel,
Saint Charles Lwanga,
Saint Perpetua and Saint Felicity,

Saint Agnes,
Saint Maria Goretti,
All holy martyrs for Christ,
Saint Leo and Saint Gregory,
Saint Ambrose,
Saint Jerome,
Saint Augustine,
Saint Athanasius,
Saint Basil and Saint Gregory,
Saint John Chrysostom,
Saint Martin,
Saint Patrick,
Saint Cyril and Saint Methodius,
Saint Charles Borromeo,
Saint Francis de Sales,
Saint Pius,
Saint Anthony,
Saint Benedict,
Saint Bernard,
Saint Francis and Saint Dominic,
Saint Thomas Aquinas,
Saint Ignatius Loyola,
Saint Francis Xavier,
Saint Vincent de Paul,
Saint John Vianney,
Saint John Bosco,
Saint Catherine,
Saint Teresa,

Saint Rose,
Saint Louis,
Saint Monica,
Saint Elizabeth,
All holy men and women,
Christ, Son of the living God,

              —Have mercy on us.

You came into this world, *(After each invocation, respond with, "Have mercy on us.")*

You suffered for us on the cross,
You died to save us,
You lay in the tomb,
You rose from the dead,
You returned in glory to the Father,
You sent the Holy Spirit upon your Apostles,
You are seated at the right hand of the Father,
You will come again to judge the living and the dead,
Lord, show us your kindness,

              —Lord, hear our prayer.

Raise our thoughts and desires to you, *(After each invocation, respond with, "Lord, hear our prayer.")*

Save us from final damnation,
Save our friends and all who have helped us,
Grant eternal rest to all who have died in the faith,
Spare us from disease, hunger and war,
Bring all peoples together in trust and peace,
Guide and protect you holy Church,
Keep the Pope and all the clergy
in faithful service to your Church,
Bring all Christians together in unity,
Lead all peoples to the light of the gospel,

Lamb of God, you take away the sins of the world,    —Have mercy on us.

Lamb of God, you take away the sins of the world,    —Have mercy on us.

Lamb of God, you take away the sins of the world,    —Have mercy on us.

Let us pray.

God of love, our strength and protection, hear the prayers of your Church.
Grant that when we come to you in faith, our prayers may be answered,
through Christ our Lord. Amen.

# Prayer to My Patron Saint

Great Saint...who at my baptism was chosen as my guardian and under whose name I became an adopted child of God and solemnly renounced Satan, his works and allurements, assist me by your powerful intercession in the fulfillment of these sacred promises.

You also made them in the days of your earthly pilgrimage, and your fidelity in keeping them to the end has obtained for you an everlasting reward in heaven.

I am called to the same happiness that you enjoy.

The same help is offered to me that enabled you to acquire eternal glory. You overcame temptations like those which I experience.

Pray for me, therefore, my holy patron, so that, being inspired by your example and assisted by your prayers, I may live a holy life, die a happy death and reach eternal life to praise and thank God in heaven with you. Amen.

# Novenas

# Novenas

The evangelist Luke recounts that after the ascension of the risen Lord, the Apostles together with Mary, the disciples and the women from Galilee spent nine days in prayer. They looked forward to a new presence of Jesus through the Spirit. These nine days of prayer and expectation led to the custom of praying for special intentions during a period of nine days. Such a period of prayer is called a novena. Novenas have become sources of inspiration and piety for people of faith who find themselves in need.

# In honor of
# Our Lady of the Miraculous Medal

*This devotion was begun by Catherine Labouré, a French religious sister. She experienced a number of apparitions of Mary. In one, Catherine saw a picture of Mary standing on a globe with light streaming from her hands. Around the Virgin were the words: "O Mary conceived without sin, pray for us who have recourse to you." Mary entrusted to Catherine the inauguration of this devotion.*

O Immaculate Virgin Mary, Mother of our Lord Jesus and our Mother, penetrated with the most lively confidence in your all-powerful and never-failing intercession, manifested so often through the Miraculous Medal, we your loving and trustful children implore you to obtain for us the graces and favors we ask during this Novena, if they be beneficial to our immortal souls, and the souls for whom we pray.

(Here privately mention your petitions.)

You know, O Mary, how often our souls have been the sanctuaries of your Son who hates iniquity.

Obtain for us then a deep hatred of sin and that purity of heart which will attach us to God alone so that our every thought, word and deed may tend to His greater glory.

Obtain for us also a spirit of prayer and self-denial that we may recover by penance what we have lost by sin and at length attain to that blessed abode where you are the Queen of angels and of men. Amen.

# An Act of Consecration to Our Lady of the Miraculous Medal

O Virgin Mother of God, Mary Immaculate, we dedicate and consecrate ourselves to you under the title of Our Lady of the Miraculous Medal.

May this Medal be for each one of us a sure sign of your affection for us and a constant reminder of our duties toward you.

Ever while wearing it, may we be blessed by your loving protection and preserved in the grace of your Son.

O most powerful Virgin, Mother of our Savior, keep us close to you every moment of our lives.

Obtain for us, your children, the grace of a happy death; so that, in union with you, we may enjoy the bliss of heaven for ever. Amen.

O Mary, conceived without sin, pray for us who have recourse to you. *(3 times.)*

# In honor of Our Lady of Fatima

*Mary appeared to three Portuguese shepherd children, Lucia, Francisco and Jacinta in 1917. She revealed herself as Our Lady of the Rosary and called for conversion in the lives of all God's people.*

Most holy Virgin, who deigned to come to Fatima, to reveal to the three little shepherds the treasures of graces hidden in the recitation of the Rosary, inspire our hearts with a sincere love of this devotion, in order that by meditating on the Mysteries of our Redemption that are recalled in it, we may gather the fruits and obtain the conversion of sinners, the conversion of Russia, and (here name the other favors you are praying for), which we ask of you in this Novena, for the greater glory of God, for your own honor, and for the good of souls. Amen.

Our Lady of the Rosary of Fatima, pray for us.

# In honor of
# Our Lady of Perpetual Help

*This title given to the Virgin Mary emphasizes her unfailing eagerness to intercede for the spiritual and temporal welfare of all of God's children, especially those who seek her intercession. This devotion is related to a fifteenth-century picture of Mary under this title which is now venerated in the Redemptorist church of Sant'Alfonso in Rome.*

O Mother of Perpetual Help, with greatest confidence I present myself to you.
I implore your help in the problems of my daily life.
Trials and sorrows often depress me; painful privations bring heartache into my life; often I meet the cross.
Have pity on me, compassionate Mother.
Take care of my needs, free me from my sufferings or if it be the will of God that I should suffer still longer, grant that I may endure all with love and patience.
Mother of Perpetual Help I ask this in your love and power.

# In honor of Our Lady of Lourdes

*The Blessed Virgin appeared at Lourdes, France to the fourteen year old Bernadette Soubirous. There were eighteen appearances between February and July, 1858. The Lady told her, "I am the Immaculate Conception." In these apparitions she called for penance. She had Bernadette drink and wash at a spring which came forth as soon as Bernadette dug and then instructed her to have a chapel built there where people could come in procession and pray.*

Be blessed, O most pure Virgin, for having vouchsafed to manifest yourself shining with life, sweetness and beauty, in the Grotto of Lourdes, saying to the child, Saint Bernadette: "I am the Immaculate Conception."

A thousand times we congratulate you upon your Immaculate Conception.

And now, O ever Immaculate Virgin, Mother of mercy, Health of the sick, Refuge of sinners, Comforter of the afflicted, you know my wants, my troubles, my sufferings; deign to cast upon me a look of mercy.

By appearing in the Grotto of Lourdes, you were pleased to make it a privileged sanctuary, whence you dispense your favors, and many have already obtained the cure of their infirmities, both spiritual and corporal. I come, therefore, with the most unbounded confidence to implore your maternal intercession.

Obtain for me, O loving Mother, the granting of my request (here mention your request). Through gratitude for your favors, I will endeavor to imitate your virtues, that I may one day share your glory.

Our Lady of Lourdes, Mother of Christ, you had influence with your Divine Son while upon earth. You have the same influence now in heaven.

Pray for me; obtain for me from your Divine Son my special request if it be Divine Will. Amen.

# In honor of
# The Immaculate Conception

*Mary is part of the mystery of Christ. Inspired by the Spirit of God, the Church grows in its understanding of this mystery and its richness. Thus the Church gradually arrives at the truth of different aspects of Mary's holiness. One such aspect is her Immaculate Conception. Mary was full of grace and free from original sin at the very beginning of her existence as a human person in her mother's womb. This was in anticipation of the merits of her Son. She was thus able to give herself wholeheartedly to her Son's person and salvific work.*

O Mary Immaculate, Lily of purity, I salute you, because from the very first instant of your conception you were filled with grace.

I thank and adore the Most Holy Trinity for having imparted such sublime favors upon you.

O Mary, full of grace, help me to share, even though just a little, in the fullness of grace so wonderfully bestowed upon you in your Immaculate Conception.

With firm confidence in your never failing intercession, we beseech you to obtain for us the intention of this novena (here mention your request), and also that purity of mind, heart and body necessary to unite us with God. Amen.

O Mary, conceved without sin, pray for us who have recourse to you.

O Mother of God, by your Immaculate Conception, intercede for us with your Divine Son, and obtain for us from Him, the favor for which we pray.

# In honor of
# Our Lady of Guadalupe

*On December 9, 1531 the Virgin Mary appeared to Juan Diego on a hill northwest of Mexico City. She disclosed to him her desire to show herself a loving mother to his people. She would be a source of consolation for all who turned to her. She instructed him to have the Bishop build a church on the site. Three days later in a second appearance she told Juan to pick flowers and take them to the Bishop. When he presented them, roses fell out of his mantle and beneath them was the painted image of the Lady. Later she said she wanted the image to be called Our Lady of Guadaloupe.*

Our Lady of Guadalupe, who blessed Mexico and all the Americas by your appearance to Juan Diego, intercede for the holy Church, protect the Pope, and help everyone who invokes you in their necessities.

O mystical rose, hear our prayers and our petitions, especially the particular one we are praying for at this moment (here mention your request).

Since you are the ever Virgin Mary and Mother of the true God, obtain for us from your most holy Son the grace of keeping our faith, sweet hope in the midst of the bitterness of life, burning charity and the precious gift of final perseverance.

We ask this through our Lord Jesus Christ, your Son, who lives and reigns with you and the Holy Spirit, one God, for ever and ever. Amen.

# In honor of Our Lady of Czestochowa

*The Blessed Virgin Mary is honored in Poland as the protectress of the Polish nation under the title of Our Lady of Czestochowa. Her image, painted in the earliest centuries of Christianity, is enshrined in a great sanctuary visited by hundreds of thousands of people over the year. The dark scars on the cheek of the Mother of God witness to the persecutions and sufferings of Poland during its long history. Under the Nazi occupation and during the Communist takeover of the nation, the image of Mary has remained a symbol of hope for a people yearning for freedom.*

Holy Mother of Czestochowa,
 full of grace and goodness,
I bring my thoughts, my words
 and actions for your blessing.
Bless my life and bless your people
 and make us free.
Give us joy amidst suffering
 and strength in persecution.
Guide our ways on earth and bring us
 to eternal life. Amen.

# In honor of Our Lady of Mount Carmel

*When the country around him was dry without water, the Prophet Elijah ascended Mount Carmel to pray for the heavens to open. Finally, he saw a small cloud coming in from the sea, bearing life-giving rain. Christian tradition would see the cloud as a symbol of Mary bringing life to a parched world. Thus Mary became honored under the title of Our Lady of Mount Carmel.*

*The English Carmelite mystic, St. Simon Stock, fostered devotion to Mary under this title. He proclaimed Mary to be a protectress of all who live honestly and justly and wear her scapular as a sign of faith in her.*

Most beautiful Mother of God,
   Splendor of heaven,
You bring fruitfulness to the earth
   and assist us in our needs.
Star of the Sea, show yourself
   a mother to me.
Let the healing rain of your comfort
   fall gently upon me.
Hear my voice when I call.
Mother of God,
I place my cause in your hands. Amen.

# In honor of the Sacred Heart of Jesus

*There was a French Visitation sister of the seventeenth century known as Margaret Mary. She was gifted with intense mystical experiences and had four visions in which Christ revealed his Sacred Heart. She heard the words, "Behold this heart which has loved so much". Christ asked that a special feast honor his love under the figure of this heart of flesh and he recommended sacramental communion on the first Friday of each month. Margaret Mary was given the task of spreading these practices. Devotion to the Sacred Heart is devotion to the person, Jesus Christ, who became man and died for our salvation.*

O Divine Jesus who said, "Ask and you shall receive; seek and you shall find; knock and it shall be opened to you," behold me prostrate at your feet.

Animated with a lively faith and confidence in these promises which are dictated by your Sacred Heart and announced by you, I come to ask (here mention your request).

Who shall I ask, O sweet Jesus, if not you, whose heart is an inexhaustable source of all graces and merits?

Where shall I seek, if not in the treasury which contains all the riches of your clemency and bounty?

Where shall I knock, if it be not at the door of your Sacred Heart, through which God Himself comes to us and through which we go to God?

To you, then, O Sacred Heart of Jesus, I have recourse.

In you I find consolation when afflicted, protection when persecuted, strength when overwhelmed with trials, and light in doubt and darkness.

I firmly believe that you can bestow upon me the graces I am asking for, even though it should require a miracle.

You only have to will it and my prayer is granted.

I know I am most unworthy of your favors O Jesus!

But this is not a reason for me to be discouraged.

You are the God of Mercy and you will not refuse a contrite and humble heart.

Look upon me with pity, I ask you, and your compassionate Heart will find in my miseries and weaknesses a reason for granting my petition.

But whatever your decision may be with regard to my request, O Sacred Heart, I will never cease to adore, praise, and serve you.

Please, dear Jesus, accept this, my act of perfect submission to the decrees of your adorable Heart, which I sincerely desire may be fulfilled in both myself and all of the faithful for ever and ever. Amen.

# In honor of the Infant of Prague

*Devotion to Jesus Christ, who came among us a child and promised that those who became like little children would enter the Kingdom of Heaven, grew in the 17th Century under the title of the Infant of Prague. A statue of the Christ Child carved of wood and covered with wax, his left hand holding a globe of the world and his right hand extended in blessing, was brought to Prague where it was enthroned in the Carmelite Church of Our Lady of Victories in 1628. Catholics have found in the image of the Christ Child a promise of God's willingness to dwell among his people in simplicity and humility and at the same time to bless our humble circumstances with the pledge of glory.*

Lord Jesus Christ, as a child you called shepherds and wise men to your crib by the light of a wonderful star. With a child's embrace you freely gave your heart and hand to all.

I come to you poor as the shepherds, seeking wisdom as the wise men. By your mighty power and gracious love grant my request.

Teach me to become like a little child and so to enter your kingdom. Give me a childlike trust in my heavenly Father who provides for me at every turn. Take from my heart the memory of wrongs that have been done to me. Renew my spirit with the joy of your youth. Bless the world you hold tenderly in your hand. Amen.

# In honor of Saint Joseph

*Saint Joseph belonged to the messianic family of David. He was a carpenter by trade and became the husband of the Virgin Mary and the foster father of Jesus. In this he received from God one of the highest vocations in the plan of redemption. The chaste personal love between himself and Mary was the human context for the growth of Jesus "in wisdom, in stature and in favor with God and men."*

O St. Joseph, whose protection is so great, so strong, so prompt before the throne of God, I place in you all my interest and desires.

O St. Joseph, do assist me by your powerful intercession, and obtain for me from your Divine Son all spiritual blessings, through Jesus Christ, our Lord.

So that, having engaged here below your heavenly power, I may offer my thanksgiving and homage to the most loving of Fathers.

O Saint Joseph, I never grow tired contemplating you, and Jesus asleep in your arms; I dare not approach while He reposes near your heart.

Press Him in my name and kiss his dear head for me and ask Him to return the kiss when I draw my dying breath. Amen.

O Saint Joseph, hear my prayers and obtain my petitions.

O Saint Joseph, pray for me.

# In honor of Saint Anne

*Nothing is known for certain about Anne, the mother of Mary. There is a legend about her that closely parallels the story of the mother of Samuel in the Old Testament. Anne, like the mother of Samuel, was childless and earnestly prayed for a child. Her prayer was answered and she saw her child as a gift of God. She thus invites believers to place their lives in the hands of God alone.*

Saint Anne, you are the mother of Mary, the Queen of heaven and earth.

During your lifetime you gave her a powerful example of love and concern.

I venerate your memory and beg your assistance.

Be concerned for me and act as my intercessor.

I ask for health of body and soul, a joyful acceptance of God's will for me and in particular (here mention your request).

Give me and those for whom I pray the strength to carry our cross in the spirit of Jesus and so live and die in his love. Amen.

# In honor of Saint Anthony of Padua

*Anthony was born near the end of the twelfth century. After ordination to the priesthood he joined the Franciscan Order. He devoted his ministry to preaching in Italy and France at a time when the church was refuting many heresies. Although he is known as the finder of lost articles, he was really one of the greatest preachers in the history of the church.*

St. Anthony, during your lifetime you were always gracious to poor sinners who sought the comfort of your ministry.

You had the happiness of holding in your arms our blessed Lord under the guise of a little child and at times the power of God enabled you to be an instrument of miraculous events.

Be gracious to me and intercede with our Lord for the petition I now make with such ardent desire (here mention your request).

As a pledge of my gratitude accept my promise to live more in harmony with the values of the Gospel and to be more devoted to the service of the poor whom you loved so deeply.
Bless this resolution and help me to be faithful. Amen.

# In honor of Saint Jude

*Jude was the apostle who asked the Lord at the Last Supper why he had manifested himself only to his disciples and not to the whole world. Postscriptural tradition asserts that Jude preached the Gospel and suffered martyrdom in Mesopotamia. In time Jude came to be regarded as the special patron of 'hopeless cases' possibly due to the fact that devotion to him had been neglected since he had the same name as the apostle who betrayed Jesus.*

St. Jude, your life was enriched with the friendship of our Lord Jesus and with his call to be one of the twelve Apostles.

The Spirit of God inspired you to write your Epistle on the Word that brings life and to witness to the truth of it by the shedding of your blood.

Obtain for me from the Giver of every good and perfect gift the graces I need.

Help me to treasure in my heart the good news of Jesus Christ and to strive by my life to bring others to its saving power. Amen.

# In honor of Saint Elizabeth Ann Seton

*Elizabeth was born in New York City, was the mother of five children and was widowed after nine years of marriage. She was received into the Catholic Church in 1805. In the course of her ministry to the poor she and her companions launched the free parochial school system. They were also the first community of the Sisters of Charity in the United States. When asked what she considered to have been the greatest grace in her life, she immediately replied, "...having been led into the Catholic Church."*

O God our Father, glorify here upon earth your servant, Saint Elizabeth Ann Seton, by manifesting the power of her intercession through the favor I now implore (here mention your request).

We ask this through our Lord Jesus Christ. Amen.

# In honor of Saint Theresa, the Little Flower

*Saint Theresa of Lisieux, France was a Carmelite sister from 1888 until her death in 1897. In the obscurity of the cloister she led a life of prayer, community living and patient suffering due to her poor health. She emphasized the 'little way' to God relating to him like a little child who trusts. In all the ordinary circumstances of her life she thus surrendered herself to the love and power of God. She is known as the Little Flower of Jesus.*

O Saint Theresa, the Little Flower of Jesus,
 please pick a rose from the heavenly garden, and send it to me with a message of love.
I beseech you to obtain for me the favors that I seek (here mention your request).
Recommend my request to Mary,
 Queen of Heaven, so that she may intercede for me, with you, before her Son, Jesus Christ.

If this favor is granted, I will love you more and more, and be better prepared to spend eternal happiness with you in heaven.

O Saint Theresa of the Little Flower, pray for me.

# Rosary Novena

*The Rosary is the most popular of the Marian devotions, and consists of three groups of five decades. They are the Joyful, the Sorrowful, and the Glorious Mysteries. The Rosary was revealed to St. Dominic by the Blessed Mother, and begun in the fifteenth century by Alan de Rupe, a Dominican preacher.*

O Mother of God, accept this Rosary
as a sign of my love and
devotion to you.
I beg you to intercede for me with
your Divine Son, and grant the favor
I so earnestly desire.
*(Here mention your request)*
O Blessed Virgin,
remember your faithful servant
by hearing my prayers and obtaining
my petitions.
O Most Holy Queen of the Rosary,
pray for me.

# The Way of the Cross

# The Way of the Cross

The Way of the Cross is a devotion in which we meditate upon the passion of Christ. Through this devotion, we can experience Jesus' suffering as he made his way to Calvary, and feel his love—a love so great that he was willing to die for both ourselves and his Father. If we can begin to understand the human experience of suffering out of love for one another, we will then begin to understand the meaning of the Cross.

# THE STATIONS OF THE CROSS

## Opening Prayer

All-loving God, I raise my mind and heart to you in praise.
Though weak and at times sinful I wish to follow your Son, Jesus, on the way of the cross.
May this meditation enable me to imitate in my own life the love with which he gave himself to you and to all his brothers and sisters.
Amen.

# FIRST STATION

### Jesus is condemned to death

The high priest then stood up before the whole assembly and put this question to Jesus, "What is this evidence these men are bringing against you?" But he was silent and made no answer at all. The high priest put a second question to him, "Are you the Christ," he said "the Son of the Blessed One?" "I am," said Jesus "and you will see the Son of Man seated at the right hand of the Power and coming with the clouds of heaven." The high priest tore his robes, "What need of witnesses have we now?" he said. "You heard the blasphemy. What is your finding?" And they all gave their verdict: he deserved to die.

*(Mk. 14, 60-64)*

Lord Jesus Crucified, have mercy on me.

# SECOND STATION

## Jesus carries his Cross

Pilate had Jesus brought out, and seated himself on the chair of judgment....
"Here is your king" said Pilate to the Jews. "Take him away, take him away!" they said. "Crucify him!" "Do you want me to crucify your king?" said Pilate. The chief priests answered, "We have no king except Caesar." So in the end Pilate handed him over to them to be crucified. They then took charge of Jesus, and carrying his own cross he went out of the city to the place of the skull or, as it was called in Hebrew, Golgotha.

*(Jn. 19, 13-17)*

Lord Jesus Crucified, have mercy on me.

# THIRD STATION

## Jesus falls the first time

Jesus said:
"If the world hates you, remember that it hated me before you. If you belonged to the world, the world would love you as its own; but because you do not belong to the world, because my choice withdrew you from the world, therefore the world hates you. Remember the words I said to you: A servant is not greater than his master. If they persecuted me, they will persecute you too."

*(Jn. 15, 18-20)*

Lord Jesus Crucified, have mercy on me.

# FOURTH STATION

**Jesus meets his afflicted mother**

Near the cross of Jesus stood his mother and his mother's sister, Mary the wife of Clopas, and Mary of Magdala. Seeing his mother and the disciple he loved standing near her, Jesus said to his mother,"Woman, this is your son". Then to the disciple he said, "This is your mother". And from that moment the disciple made a place for her in his home.

*(Jn. 19, 25-27)*

Lord Jesus Crucified, have mercy on me.

# FIFTH STATION

**Simon of Cyrene helps Jesus to carry his Cross**

And when the soldiers had finished making fun of him, they took off the purple and dressed him in his own clothes. They led him out to crucify him. They enlisted a passerby, Simon of Cyrene, father of Alexander and Rufus, who was coming in from the country, to carry his cross. They brought Jesus to the place called Golgotha, which means the place of the skull.

*(Mk. 15, 20-22)*

Lord Jesus Crucified, have mercy on me

# SIXTH STATION

## Veronica wipes the face of Jesus

The King will say to those on his right hand, "Come, you whom my Father has blessed, take for your heritage the kingdom prepared for you since the foundation of the world... The virtuous will say to him in reply, "Lord, when did we see you hungry and feed you; or thirsty and give you drink? When did we see you a stranger and make you welcome; naked and clothe you; sick or in prison and go to see you?" And the King will answer, "I tell you solemnly, in so far as you did this to one of the least of these brothers of mine, you did it to me."

*(Mt. 25, 34, 37-40)*

Lord Jesus Crucified, have mercy on me.

# SEVENTH STATION

### Jesus falls the second time

Ours were the sufferings he bore, ours the sorrows he carried. But we, we thought of him as someone punished, struck by God, and brought low. Yet he was pierced through for our faults, crushed for our sins. On him lies a punishment that brings us peace, and through his wounds we are healed.

We had all gone astray like sheep, each taking his own way, and Yahweh burdened him with the sins of all of us.

*(Is. 53, 4-6)*

Lord Jesus Crucified, have mercy on me.

# EIGHTH STATION

## Jesus meets the women of Jerusalem

Large numbers of people followed him, and of women too, who mourned and lamented for him. But Jesus turned to them and said, "Daughters of Jerusalem, do not weep for me; weep rather for yourselves and for your children."

*(Lk. 23, 27-28)*

Lord Jesus Crucified, have mercy on me.

# NINTH STATION

## Jesus falls a third time

Jesus said,
I have come from heaven,
not to do my own will,
but to do the will of the one who sent me.
Now the will of him who sent me
is that I should lose nothing
of all that he has given to me,
and that I should raise it up on the
   last day.

*(Jn. 6, 38-39)*

Lord Jesus Crucified, have mercy on me.

# TENTH STATION

## Jesus is stripped of his clothes

They gave him wine to drink mixed with gall, which he tasted but refused to drink. When the soldiers had finished crucifying Jesus they took his clothing and divided it into four shares, one for each soldier. His undergarment was seamless, woven in one piece from neck to hem; so they said to one another, "Instead of tearing it, let's throw dice to decide who is to have it." In this way the words of scripture were fulfilled:
'They shared out my clothing among
 them.
They cast lots for my clothes.'
This is exactly what the soldiers did.
*(Mt. 27, 34-35)*

Lord Jesus Crucified, have mercy on me.

# ELEVENTH STATION

## Jesus is nailed to the Cross

At the place called The Skull, they crucified him there and the two criminals also, one on the right, the other on the left. Jesus said, "Father, forgive them; they do not know what they are doing"... The people stayed there watching him. As for the leaders, they jeered at him. "He saved others," they said "let him save himself if he is the Christ of God, the Chosen One." The soldiers mocked him too, and when they approached to offer him vinegar they said, "If you are the King of the Jews, save yourself". Above him there was an inscription: "This is the king of the Jews".

*(Lk. 23, 33-38)*

Lord Jesus Crucified, have mercy on me.

# TWELFTH STATION

### Jesus dies on the Cross

It was now about the sixth hour and, with the sun eclipsed, a darkness came over the whole land until the ninth hour. The veil of the Temple was torn right down the middle; and when Jesus had cried out in a loud voice, he said, "Father, into your hands I commit my spirit." With these words he breathed his last.

*(Lk. 23, 44-46)*

Lord Jesus Crucified, have mercy on me.

# THIRTEENTH STATION

**The body of Jesus
is taken down from the Cross**

When the soldiers came to Jesus, they found he was already dead, and so instead of breaking his legs one of the soldiers pierced his side with a lance; and immediately there came out blood and water... After this, Joseph of Arimathaea, who was a disciple of Jesus—though a secret one because he was afraid of the Jews—asked Pilate to let him remove the body of Jesus. Pilate gave permission, so they came and took it away.

*(Jn. 19, 33-34 38)*

Lord Jesus Crucified, have mercy on me.

# FOURTEENTH STATION

## Jesus is laid in the tomb

So Joseph took the body, wrapped it in a clean shroud and put it in his own new tomb which he had hewn out of the rock. He then rolled a large stone across the entrance of the tomb and went away.
*(Mt. 27, 59-60)*

Lord Jesus Crucified, have mercy on me.

# FIFTEENTH STATION

## The Resurrection of Jesus

*A new tradition has arisen in the devotion of the Way of the Cross. A "Fifteenth Station" has been added to show how the sufferings of Jesus and the glory of his resurrection are inseparably joined in the Paschal Mystery.*
*By dying he destroyed our death and by rising again he restored us to life.*

When the sabbath was over, Mary of Magdala, Mary the mother of James, and Salome, bought spices with which to go and anoint him. And very early in the morning on the first day of the week they went to the tomb, just as the sun was rising.

They had been saying to one another, "Who will roll away the stone for us from the entrance to the tomb?" But when they looked they could see that the stone—which was very big—had already been rolled back. On entering the tomb they saw a young man in a white robe seated on the right-hand side, and they were struck with amazement. But he said to them, "There is no need for alarm. You are looking for Jesus of Nazareth, who was crucified; he has risen, he is not here. See, here is the place where they laid him."

*Mk. 16, 1-6)*

## Closing Prayer

Heavenly Father,
   I thank you for calling me to glory
   in Jesus our Savior.
May the remembrance of his passion,
   death and resurrection
   sustain me on my earthly pilgrimage.
May his example strengthen me in
   faith, hope and love. Amen.

# Meditation

JESUS' STORY does not end in sadness but in gladness. He not only died, but on Easter Sunday he rose out of his tomb gloriously alive.

Jesus' Father, who is God, willed to allow Jesus to die out of love for us—to give everything he had for us. He also willed to bring Jesus back to life so that in Jesus we have no need to fear death. Jesus will lead us through death to new life.

# Prayers to the Blessed Virgin Mary

# The Regina Caeli

### "Queen of Heaven"

Queen of heaven, rejoice, Alleluia.
 The Son whom you were privileged to bear,
 Alleluia, has risen as he said, Alleluia.
Pray to God for us, Alleluia.
Rejoice and be glad, Virgin Mary, Alleluia.
 For the Lord has truly risen. Alleluia.

Let us pray. O God
 it was by the Resurrection of your Son, our Lord Jesus Christ,
 that you brought joy to the world.
Grant that through the intercession of the Virgin Mary, his Mother, we may attain the joy of eternal life.
Through Christ, our Lord. Amen.

# The Angelus

The angel of the Lord declared unto Mary.
And she conceived of the Holy Spirit. Hail Mary...
Behold the handmaid of the Lord.
Be it done unto me according to your word. Hail Mary...
And the Word was made flesh; and dwelt among us. Hail Mary...
Pray for us, O holy Mother of God, that we may be made worthy of the promises of Christ.

Let us pray.
Pour forth, we beseech You, O Lord, your grace in our hearts, that we, to whom the incarnation of Christ, Your Son, was made known by the message of an angel, may by his Passion and Cross be brought to the glory of his Resurrection; through the same Christ our Lord. Amen.

# The Memorare

Remember, O most gracious Virgin Mary,
  that never was it known that
  anyone who fled to your protection,
  implored your help,
  or sought your intercession
  was left unaided.
Inspired by this confidence,
  we fly unto you, O Virgin of virgins,
  our Mother!
To you we come, before you we stand,
  sinful and sorrowful.
O Mother of the Word incarnate,
  despise not our petitions, but
  in your mercy hear and answer us.
  Amen.

# Prayer of St. Alphonsus Liguori

O Most holy and Immaculate Virgin, my Mother; you are the Mother of my Lord, the Queen of the world, the advocate, hope, and refuge of sinners, and I, the most miserable of those sinners, come to you today.

I venerate you, great Queen, and thank you for the many graces that you have bestowed upon me, and I especially want to thank you for having saved me so many times from the punishment of God, a punishment which I deserved.

I love you, most lovable Lady, and by the love I have for you, I promise that I will always serve you and do as much as I can to make others love you.

I put all of my hope and my entire salvation in you.

Receive me as your servant, O Mother of Mercy, and cover me with the mantle of your protection.

Since you are so powerful with God, free me from all temptations or, at least, obtain the graces for me to overcome them until death.

I ask of you a true love for Jesus Christ, and through you I hope to die a good death. My Mother, by the love you have for God, I beg you to always help me, especially at the last moment of my life.

Do not leave me until you see me safe in heaven.

I hope to thank and praise you there for ever.

# Prayer of St. Francis de Sales

O most Holy Mary, Virgin Mother of God, even though I am most unworthy to be your servant, I am moved by your motherly care for me and long to serve you.

I choose you this day to be my Queen, my Advocate and my Mother, and I firmly resolve to always be devoted to you and to do what I can to encourage others to be devoted to you.

My loving Mother, through the Precious Blood of your Son that was shed for me, I beg you to receive me as your eternal servant.

Aid me in my actions and beg for me the grace never by word, deed or thought to be displeasing in either your sight or that of your most holy Son.

Remember me, dearest Mother, and do not abandon me at the hour of my death.

# Prayer of St. Louis de Montfort

Hail Mary, beloved Daughter of the eternal Father, wonderful Mother of the Son, faithful Spouse of the Holy Spirit.

You are my loving Lady, my powerful Queen.

You are all mine through your mercy, and I am all yours.

Take away everything from me that may be displeasing to God.

Cultivate in me everything that is pleasing to you.

May the light of your faith dispel the darkness of my mind, your deep humility replace my pride; your continual sight of God fill my memory with his presence; and the fire of your heart. inflame the lukewarmness of my own heart.

May your virtues take the place of my sins, and may your merits be my enrichment to make up for all that is wanting in me before God.

My beloved Mother, grant that I may have no other spirit than yours, that I know Jesus Christ and His Divine Will and that I glorify the Lord. Hail Mary, my dear Mother, may I love God with a burning love like yours.

## Prayer of St. Thomas Aquinas

O Virgin full of goodness, the Mother of mercy, I entrust my body and soul, my thoughts, my actions, and my life and death to you.

O my Queen, help me, and deliver me from the grasp of the devil. Obtain for me the grace of loving my Lord Jesus Christ, your Son, with a true and perfect love.

And after Him, O Mary, obtain for me that same grace, so that I may love you with all my heart and above all things.

# The Thirty Days' Prayer to the Blessed Virgin Mary

Ever glorious and blessed Mary, Queen of Virgins, mother of mercy, hope and comfort of dejected and desolate souls, through that sword of sorrow which pierced your tender heart, while your only Son, Jesus Christ, our Lord, suffered death and ignominy on the Cross; through that filial tenderness and pure love he had for you, grieving in your sorrows, while from His cross he recommended you to the care and protection of his beloved disciple, St. John; take pity I beseech you, on my poverty and necessities; have compassion on my anxieties and cares; assist and comfort me in all my infirmities and miseries.

You are the mother of mercies, the sweet consolatrix and refuge of the needy and the orphan, of the desolate and the afflicted.

Cast, therefore, an eye of pity on a miserable, forlorn child of Eve, and hear my prayer, for since, in just punishment of my sins, I may find myself encompassed by a multitude of evils, and oppressed with much anguish of spirit, whither can I fly for more secure shelter, O amiable Mother of my Lord and Savior, Jesus Christ, than under the wings of your maternal protection?

Attend, therefore, I beseech you, with an air of pity and compassion, to my humble and earnest request.

I ask it through the mercy of your dear Son, through that love and condescension with which he embraced our nature, when, in compliance with the divine will, you gave your consent; and whom, after the expiration of nine months, you did bring forth from your chaste womb, to visit this world, and bless it with his presence.

I ask it through the anguish of mind with which your beloved Son, our dear Savior, was overwhelmed on Mt.

Olivet, when he besought his eternal Father, to remove from him, if possible, the bitter chalice of his future Passion.

I ask it through the threefold repetition of his prayer in the garden, whence afterwards with sorrowful steps and mournful tears, you did accompany him to the doleful theatre of his death and sufferings.

I ask it through the stripes and sores of his virginal flesh, occasioned by the cords and whips with which he was bound and scourged, when stripped of his seamless garment for which his executioners afterwards cast lots.

I ask it through the scoffs and ignominies by which he was insulted, the false accusations and unjust sentence by which he was condemned to death, and which he bore with heavenly patience.

I ask it through his bitter tears and bloody sweat, his silence and resignation, his sadness and grief of heart.

I ask it through the blood which trickled from his royal and sacred head when struck with the sceptre of a reed and pierced with his crown of thorns.

I ask it through his vehement thirst and bitter potion of vinegar and gall.

I ask it through his dereliction on the cross, when he exclaimed:

"My God! My God! Why hast Thou forsaken me?"

I ask it through his mercy, extended to the repentant thief; and through his recommending his precious soul and spirit into the hands of his eternal Father, before he expired, saying, "All is consummated."

I ask it through the blood mixed with water, which issued from his sacred side when pierced with a lance, and whence a flood of grace and mercy has flowed to us.

I ask it through his immaculate life, bitter Passion, and ignominious death on the cross, at which nature itself was thrown into convulsions, by the bursting of rocks, rending of the veil of the temple, the earthquake and darkness of the sun and moon.

I ask it through his descent into hell where he comforted the Saints of the Old Testament with his presence, and led captivity captive.

I ask it through his glorious victory over death, when he arose again to life on the third day; and through the joy which his appearance for forty days after gave you, his blessed Mother, his Apostles, and the rest of his disciples, when, in thine and their presence, he miraculously ascended into heaven.

I ask it through the grace of the Holy Spirit, infused into the hearts of his disciples, when he descended upon them in the form of fiery tongues, and by which they were inspired with zeal in the conversion of the world, when they went to preach the Gospel.

I ask it through the awful appearance of your Son at the last dreadful day, when he shall come to judge the living and the dead, and destroy the world by fire.

I ask it through the compassion he bore you in this life and the ineffable joy you did feel at your Assumption into heaven, where you are eternally absorbed in the sweet contemplation of his divine perfections.

O Glorious and everblessed Virgin, comfort the heart of your suppliant, by obtaining for me:

*(Here mention or reflect on your request)*

And as I am persuaded, my divine Savior does honor you as his beloved Mother, to whom he refuses nothing, because you ask nothing contrary to his honor, so let me speedily experience the efficacy of your powerful intercession, according to the tenderness of your maternal affection, and his filial, loving heart, who mercifully grants the requests, and complies with the desires of those that love and fear him.
Wherefore, O most Blessed Virgin, besides the object of my present petition, and whatever else I may stand in need of, obtain for me also of your dear Son, our Lord and our God, a lively faith, a firm hope, perfect charity, true contrition of heart, a horror of sin, love of God and my neighbor, contempt of the world, patience to suffer affronts and ignominies: and,

even, if necessary, an opprobrious death itself, for love of your Son, our Savior, Jesus Christ.

Obtain for me likewise, O sacred Mother of God, perseverance in good works, performance of good resolutions, mortification of self-will, a pious conversation through life and, at my last moments, strong and sincere repentance, accompanied with such a lively and attentive presence of mind, as may enable me worthily to receive the last Sacraments of the Church, and die in your friendship and favor.

Lastly, obtain, I beseech you, for the souls of my parents, brethren, relatives, and benefactors, both living and dead, life everlasting. Amen.

# The Rosary of the Blessed Virgin Mary

# The Rosary of the Blessed Virgin Mary

"The devotion of the Rosary contributes greatly to the destruction of sin, the recovery of grace, and the promotion of the glory of God."

*Gregory XVI*

*The Rosary is the most popular of all the Marian devotions. It was revealed to St. Dominic by the Blessed Mother, and begun in the fifteenth century by Alan de Rupe, a Dominican preacher. The Rosary combines both vocal and meditative prayer, and is treasured by all who use it.*

*The complete Rosary consists of fifteen decades, but is further divided into three distinct parts, each containing five decades; called the Joyful, the Sorrowful, and the Glorious Mysteries. The Mysteries of the Rosary symbolize important events from the lives of both our Lord and the Blessed Mother.*

*Each decade contains one mystery, an "Our Father," ten "Hail Marys," and a "Glory be to the Father." To say the Rosary, begin by making the sign of the cross and saying "The Apostles' Creed" on the crucifix, one "Our Father" on the first bead, three "Hail Marys" on the next three beads, and then a "Glory be to the Father." When this is finished, meditate upon the first mystery, say an "Our Father," ten "Hail Marys," and one "Glory be to the Father." The first decade is now completed, and to finish the Rosary proceed in the same manner until all five decades have been said.*

# The Five Joyful Mysteries

(Mondays and Thursdays)

1. *The Annunciation*—The Angel Gabriel tells Mary that she is to be the Mother of God. (Humility)
2. *The Visitation*—The Blessed Virgin pays a visit to her cousin Elizabeth. (Charity)
3. *The Nativity*—The Infant Jesus is born in a stable at Bethlehem. (Poverty)
4. *The Presentation*—The Blessed Virgin presents the Child Jesus to Simeon in the temple. (Obedience)
5. *The Finding in the Temple*—Jesus is lost for three days, and the Blessed Mother finds him in the Temple. (Piety)

# The Five Sorrowful Mysteries

(Tuesdays and Fridays)

1. *The Agony in the Garden*—Jesus prays in the Garden of Olives and drops of blood break through his skin. (Contrition)

2. *The Scourging at the Pillar*—Jesus is tied to a pillar and cruelly beaten with whips. (Purity)

3. *The Crowning with Thorns*—A crown of thorns is placed upon Jesus' head. (Courage)

4. *The Carrying of the Cross*—Jesus is made to carry his cross to Calvary. (Patience)

5. *The Crucifixion*—Jesus is nailed to the cross, and dies for our sins. (Self-denial)

# The Five Glorious Mysteries

(Wednesdays, Saturdays and Sundays)

1. *The Resurrection*—Jesus rises from the dead, three days after his death. (Faith)

2. *The Ascension*—Forty days after his death, Jesus ascends into heaven. (Hope)

3. *The Descent of the Holy Spirit*—Ten days after the ascension, the Holy Spirit comes to the apostles and the Blessed Mother in the form of fiery tongues. (Love)

4. *The Assumption*—The Blessed Virgin dies and is assumed into heaven. (Eternal Happiness)

5. *The Crowning of the Blessed Virgin*—The Blessed Virgin is crowned Queen of Heaven and Earth by Jesus, her son. (Devotion to Mary)

# Hail, Holy Queen

*Originally a hymn, this prayer dates back to the eleventh century. It is sometimes said at the end of the Rosary, as is the Litany of the Blessed Virgin Mary, which can be found on page 142.*

Hail, holy Queen, mother of mercy, our life, our sweetness, and our hope.
To you do we cry, poor banished children of Eve; to you we send up our sighs, mourning and weeping in this valley of tears.
Turn then, O most gracious advocate, your eyes of mercy toward us, and after this our exile, show unto us the blessed fruit of your womb, Jesus.
O clement, O loving, O sweet Virgin Mary.

> V. Pray for us, O holy Mother of God.
> R. That we may be made worthy of the promises of Christ.

Let us pray.

O God, whose only begotten Son, by his life, death, and Resurrection, has purchased for us the rewards of eternal life, grant, we beseech you, that meditating upon these Mysteries of the most Holy Rosary of the Blessed Virgin Mary, we may imitate what they contain and obtain what they promise.

Through the same Christ our Lord. Amen.

# Devotion of the Five First Saturdays

# Devotion of the Five First Saturdays

*The Blessed Mother appeared on six occasions to three children near the village of Fatima in Portugal, from May 13th to October 13th in 1917. Upon the last occasion, Our Lady performed a great miracle.*

*In so doing, the Blessed Virgin confirmed by an outward sign, her appearance to institute the devotion to her Immaculate Heart. Our Lady promised that if her requests were heard, Russia would be converted, there would be peace in the world and salvation for all sinners. This would be accomplished by devotion to both her Immaculate Heart, through the daily Rosary, and the Five First Saturdays.*

*The three children who saw Our Lady were Francisco and Jacinta Marto, and their cousin, Lucia Dos Santos. In 1925, Lucia joined the convent of the Sisters of St. Dorothy in Tuy, Spain, under the name of Sr. Marie of the Sorrows. On December 10, 1925, the Blessed Virgin appeared to Sister Marie in her room, and revealed her Immaculate Heart. Our Lady asked Sr. Marie to reveal this message to the world:*

"I promise to assist at the hour of death with the graces necessary for salvation, all those who on the First Saturday of five consecutive months, confess, receive Holy Communion, recite five decades of my Rosary, and keep me company for a quarter of an hour while meditating on the mysteries of the Rosary, with the intention of offering me reparation."

## The Prayers of Fatima

*On July 13, 1917, Our Lady taught this prayer to the children. It is to be recited after each decade of the rosary.*

O my Jesus, forgive us. Deliver us from the fire of hell. Draw the souls of all to heaven, especially those in greatest need.

*Of the following prayer, Our Lady said: "Say many times and especially when you make any sacrifices":*

O Jesus, it is for Your love, for the conversion of sinners, and in reparation for the sins committed against the Immaculate Heart of Mary.

*As a prelude to the appearances of Our Lady, the children received a visitation from the guardian angel of Portugal. He taught them the following prayer:*

My God, I believe, I adore, I hope, and I love You. I ask pardon for those who do not believe, do not adore, do not hope, and do not love You.

*The angel also taught them this prayer, which they recited on their knees, with their foreheads touching the ground:*

Most Holy Trinity, Father, Son, and Holy Spirit, I adore You profoundly, and I offer You the most precious body, blood, soul, and divinity of Jesus Christ present in all the tabernacles of the world in reparation for the outrages, sacrileges, and indifferences with which He is offended, and by the infinite merits of His Most Sacred Heart and of the Immaculate Heart of Mary I ask You for the conversion of poor sinners.

# Feasts of The Blessed Virgin Mary

# Feasts of
# The Blessed Virgin Mary

| | |
|---|---|
| January 1: | **Solemnity of Mary, The Mother of God** |
| February 2: | **Presentation of Jesus in the Temple** |
| February 11: | **Our Lady of Lourdes** |
| March 25: | **The Annunciation** |
| May 31: | **The Visitation** <br> **The Immaculate Heart of Mary** |
| July 16: | **Our Lady of Mt. Carmel** |
| August 5: | **Dedication of St. Mary Major** |
| August 15: | **The Assumption of the Blessed Virgin Mary** |
| August 22: | **The Queenship of Mary** |
| September 8: | **The Birth of Mary** |
| September 15: | **Our Lady of Sorrows** |
| October 7: | **Our Lady of the Rosary** |

| | |
|---|---|
| November 21: | **The Presentation of Mary** |
| December 8: | **The Immaculate Conception** |
| December 12: | **Our Lady of Guadalupe** |
| December 25: | **Christmas, The Birth of Our Lord** |

# Prayers to St. Joseph

# Prayer to Saint Joseph

Loving Saint Joseph, may your holy life be an inspiration to me when I find it difficult to be faithful in the fulfillment of my duties.

You are now glorified with Jesus and Mary and are a powerful intercessor at the throne of God.

Blessed foster-father of Jesus, extend to me the same tender care with which you protected Jesus and Mary that I may walk securely in the path of salvation.

Obtain for me strong faith, ardent love and zeal in doing good. With Jesus and Mary, help me at the hour of my death so that I may partake of the complete redemption of the children of God and eternally praise the Father, Son, and Holy Spirit. Amen.

# Prayer to Saint Joseph, the Worker

Glorious Saint Joseph, model of all who are dedicated to labor, obtain for me the grace to work in the spirit of love and to faithfully place my responsibilities above my own desires.

Help me to work with joy and gratitude.

Let me consider it an honor to use and develop the gifts I have received from God.

Aid me to work with order, peace, moderation and patience.

Help me to work above all for the glory of God and the coming of his kingdom.

May I remember that I am to give an account of the gifts and talents I have received.

# Prayer to Saint Joseph for Others

Saint Joseph, be my patron and intercessor with God.

Through the merits of Jesus and Mary obtain for me pardon of all my sins.

Implore for me a great purity of heart, a lively faith, firm hope and perfect charity.

Help me in all my needs of soul and body but most of all in the hour of my death.

Come to me then with Jesus and Mary and let me die in their love and with the help of your prayers.

Glorious Saint Joseph, powerful protector of holy Church, I implore your heavenly aid for the whole Church on earth, especially for the Holy Father and all bishops, priests and religious.

Guide and help all government officials, comfort the afflicted, console the dying, and convert sinners. Have pity on all who have died especially members of my own family and friends.

Allow them to join you and all the saints in the praise and glory of God. Amen.

# Prayer to Saint Joseph for Strength

Saint Joseph we confidently invoke your patronage.

By that charity with which you were united to the immaculate virgin mother of God and by that fatherly love with which you embraced the child Jesus, we beg you and humbly pray that you will look graciously upon the inheritance which Jesus Christ purchased by his blood and assist us in our need by your power and strength.

Most watchful guardian of the holy family, protect the chosen people of Jesus Christ.

Keep far from us, most loving father, all blight of error and corruption.

Mercifully help us from heaven, most valiant defender, in this conflict with the powers of darkness. And even as of old you rescued the child Jesus from the peril of his life, so now defend God's holy church from the snares of the enemy and from all adversity.

Keep us one and all under your continual protection, that supported by your example and your help, we may lead a holy life, die a happy death and come at last to the possession of everlasting blessedness in heaven.
> Amen.

## Prayer to Saint Joseph, the Guardian

O Blessed Saint Joseph, faithful guardian and protector of virgins, to whom God entrusted Jesus and Mary, I implore you by the love
which you did bear them,
to preserve me from every defilement of soul and body,
that I may always serve them in holiness and purity of love. Amen.

# Prayer to Saint Joseph

O Holy Joseph, chaste spouse of the Mother of God, most glorious advocate of all who are in danger or in their last agony, and most faithful protector of all the servants of Mary, I, in the presence of Jesus and Mary, do from this moment choose you for my powerful patron and advocate, and I implore you to obtain for me through your powerful intercession the grace of a happy death.

Receive me, therefore, for your perpetual servant, and recommend me to the constant protection of Mary, your spouse, and to the everlasting mercies of Jesus, my Savior.

Assist me in all the actions of my life, which I now offer to the greater glory of Jesus and Mary.

Never, therefore, forsake me; and whatsoever grace you see most necessary and profitable for me, obtain it for me now and also at the hour of my death.

I know not when I shall die, but in whatsoever hour it shall happen I invite you to be with me at my deathbed.

Through your gracious intercession may there be granted me in my last hour all the graces I need, through the merits of Jesus Christ, my Savior, who together with the Father and the Holy Spirit, lives and reigns, world without end. Amen.

# Prayer to Saint Joseph

*Especially recommended to be said with the Rosary during October*

To you, O blessed Joseph,
 we have recourse in our affliction;
 and having implored the help of your
 most holy Spouse, we confidently
 invoke your patronage also.
By that charity which bound you
 to the Immaculate Virgin,
 Mother of God,
 and by the fatherly love with
 which you embraced the Child Jesus,
 look down, we beseech you,
 with gracious eye on the precious
 inheritance which Jesus Christ
 purchased in his blood,
 and help us in our necessities
 by your power and aid.
Protect, O most watchful Guardian
 of the Holy Family,
 the elect children of Jesus Christ;
 ward off from us,
 O most loving Father,
 all blight of error and corruption;
 aid us from on high,

O most valiant Defender, in our
struct struggle with the powers of darkness;
and, even as of old
you rescued the Child Jesus
from the greatest peril of his life,
so now defend God's Holy Church
from the snares of the enemy and
from all adversity.
Shield also each one of us
by your constant protection, so that,
supported by your example and
your aid, we may live a holy life,
die a happy death, and attain
everlasting happiness in heaven.
Amen.

# Thanksgiving Prayers

# Thanksgiving Prayers

Father of all gifts, we praise you, the source of all we have and are.
  Teach us to acknowledge always the good things your infinite love has given us.
Help us to love you with all our hearts and all our strength as our expression of thanksgiving for your many blessings.
Fill our hearts with this spirit of gratitude. Amen.

Father of mercy, we thank you for your kindness and ask you to free us from all evil that we may serve you with generous hearts and in happiness all our days.
Make us always aware of your mercies that with truly thankful hearts, we may make known your praise by giving wholeheartedly of ourselves, and by true holiness of lives all honor and glory will be yours throughout all ages. Amen.

Almighty God, Father of all mercies, we your unworthy servants give you humble thanks for all your goodness and loving kindness to us and to all men.

We bless you for our creation and all the blessings of this life, but above all, for your incomparable and undying love in the redemption of the world by your Son, our Lord and Savior Jesus Christ. Amen.

Heavenly Father, we your unworthy servants give you humble thanks for all your goodness and loving kindness to us and to all men, particularly our families, friends and loved ones. Amen.

# Te Deum

O God, we praise You, and acknowledge You to be the supreme Lord.
Everlasting Father, all the earth worships You.
All the angels, the heavens and all angelic powers, all the cherubim and seraphim, continually cry to You:
Holy, holy, holy, Lord God of Hosts!
Heaven and earth are full of the majesty of Your glory.
The glorious choir of the apostles,
The wonderful company of prophets,
The white-robed army of martyrs, praise You.
Holy Church throughout the world acknowledges You:
The Father of infinite majesty;
Your adorable, true and only Son;
Also the Holy Spirit, the Comforter.
O Christ, You are the King of Glory!
You are the everlasting Son of the Father.
When You took it upon Yourself to deliver man,
You did not disdain the Virgin's womb.

Having overcome the sting of death, You opened the kingdom of heaven to all believers.

You sit at the right hand of God in the glory of the Father.

We believe that You will come to be our Judge.

We, therefore, beg You to help Your servants whom You have redeemed with Your Precious Blood.

Let them be numbered with Your saints in everlasting glory.

Save your people, O Lord, and bless Your inheritance!

Govern them, and raise them up forever.

Every day we thank You.

And we praise Your name forever; yes, forever and ever.

O Lord, deign to keep us from sin this day.

Have mercy on us, O Lord, have mercy on us.

Let Your mercy, O Lord, be upon us, for we have hoped in You.

O Lord, in You I have put my trust; let me never be put to shame.

# Prayer of Adoration

I adore you, O God.
   I count myself as nothing before your
divine majesty.
   You alone are life, truth, beauty and
goodness.
   I glorify you, I praise you, I give you
thanks and I love you,
   helpless and unworthy as I am,
   in union with your dear son
   Jesus Christ,
   our saviour and our brother.
   I desire to serve you, to please you,
   to obey you and to love you always
   in union with Mary Immaculate,
   Mother of God and our mother.
Give me your Holy Spirit
   to enlighten me,
   to correct me and
   to guide me
   in the way of your commandments
   and in all perfection,
   while I look for the happiness of
heaven, where I shall glorify you
for ever and ever. Amen.

# Peace Prayers

## Prayers for Peace

God our Father, you reveal that those who work for peace will be called your sons.
Help us to work without ceasing for that justice which brings true and everlasting peace.
We ask this through Christ our Lord. Amen.

God, Creator of the world, you established the order which governs all ages.
Hear our prayer and give us peace in our time that we may rejoice in your mercy and praise you without end.
We ask this through Jesus, your Son and our Lord. Amen.

God of perfect peace, neither violence nor cruelty can be part of you.
May those who are at peace with one another hold fast to the good will that unites them.

May those who are enemies forget their hatred and be healed.
Grant this peace to all men throughout the world. Amen.

Lord Jesus Christ, we praise you; bring peace into the world by bringing your peace into the hearts of men.
Help us to turn away from sin, and to follow you in love and service.
Glory and honor be yours for ever and ever. Amen.

## A Family's Prayer for World Peace

Lord Jesus Christ,
who said to your apostles:
"Peace I leave with you,
my peace I give to you;
not as the world gives,
do I give to you,"
regard not our sins but your merits.
Grant to all your servants that they,
whom the almighty Father has created
and governs and whom you have

redeemed by your precious blood and
destined for everlasting life
may love one another
with all their hearts for your sake
and may be made one in spirit and
rejoice in your perpetual peace.
Lord Jesus Christ,
concerning whom the prophet has said:
"And all kings of the earth shall adore
him, all nations shall serve him,"
extend your reign over the whole
human race.
Send upon all men
the light of your faith,
deliver them from all the snares and
bonds of passion and
direct them to heavenly things.
Graciously grant that states and nations
may be united through your holy
Church and through the intercession
of the blessed virgin Mary,
queen of peace,
that they may serve you in all humility;
and that all tongues and peoples
may form one great choir to praise you
king and ruler of the nations,
prince of peace, immortal king of ages.
Amen.

# Special Prayers

## For the Church

Father, in the new covenant instituted by Christ your Son, you gather your people in the unity of your Spirit from all the nations of the earth.
Keep your Church faithful to her mission as a leaven in the world, renewing all peoples in Christ and transforming them into your own family. Amen.

## For the Pope

Father, as successor to the Apostle, Peter, you have chosen your servant to be the vicar of Christ on earth and shepherd of the whole flock.
May he strengthen his brothers, and may the whole Church be in communion with him in the bond of unity, love and peace, that all men may receive from you, the shepherd and bishop of their souls, truth and eternal life. Amen.

### For the Church Under Persecution

Father, in the mystery of your providence the Church was to share in the sufferings of Christ your Son.
Give those who suffer persecution for their faith a share also in the patience and love of your Son, that they may be true and faithful witnesses to his promise of resurrection and eternal life. Amen.

### For the Local Church

Father, in each and every local Church, pilgrims here on earth, you show forth your one, holy, catholic and apostolic Church.
Gathered around its shepherd may this family grow in the love and unity of the Holy Spirit through the Gospel and the Eucharist.
Make us become a true witness to the presence of Christ in the world. Amen.

## For the Bishop

God our Father, you have entrusted to
 your servant N., as a successor to the
 Apostles, the care of the diocese of...
Give him your Spirit of wisdom and
 courage, of understanding and love.
Keep him faithful to his mission that
 he may build up your Church, the
 universal sacrament of salvation.
 Amen.

## For Priests

Father, you appointed your only Son as
 the eternal high priest.
Grant that those he has chosen to be
 ministers of word and sacament may
 be faithful in their ministry until the
 day of his coming. Amen.

## For Religious

Father, every good intention has its origin and fulfillment in you.
Guide your people along the path of salvation and look kindly on those who have left all things to follow Christ in chastity, poverty and obedience and to consecrate themselves to you.
In their service to you, Father, and to all their brothers and sisters, may they give faithful witness to Christ. Amen.

## For the Unity of Christians

God our Father, bring the hearts of all believers together in praise of you and in seeking renewal and reconciliation.
May the divisions between Christians be overcome.
Make us one in faith and love as we walk with Christ to the joy of your eternal kingdom. Amen.

### For the Missions

God of truth, Father, Son, and Holy Spirit, hear our prayer for those who do not know you, that your name may be praised among all peoples of the world.
Sustain and inspire your servants who bring them the Gospel.
Bring fresh vigor to wavering faith; sustain our faith when it is still fragile.
Renew our missionary zeal.
Make us witnesses to your goodness, full of love, of strength and of faith, for your glory and for the salvation of the world. Amen.

### For the Sick

Father, your only Son took upon himself the sufferings and weakness of all mankind; through his passion and cross he taught us how good can be brought out of suffering.
Look upon our brothers and sisters who are ill.
In the midst of illness and pain, may they be united with Christ, who heals both

body and soul; may they know the consolation promised to those who suffer and be fully restored to health. Amen.

## For Those Who are Suffering

Father, you are the unfailing refuge of those who suffer.
Bring peace and comfort to the sick and the infirm, to the aged and the dying.
Give all those who look after them knowledge, patience, and compassion.
Inspire them with actions which will bring relief, words which will enlighten, and love which will bring comfort.
We commend to you the disheartened, the rebellious, those torn by temptation or tormented by desire, and those wounded or abused by the ill will of men.
Lord, pour out on us your Spirit of love, understanding and sacrifice; may we then give effective help to the suffering we meet on our way.
Help us to answer their cry, for it is our own. Amen.

### For the Aged

Eternal Father, unchanged down the changing years, be near to those who are aged.
Even though their bodies weaken, grant that their spirit may be strong; may they bear weariness and affliction with patience, and, at the end, meet death with serenity. Amen.


### Prayer for Charity in the Family

O Lord, our God, we offer you our hearts united in the strongest and most sincere love of brotherhood.
We pray that Jesus may be the daily food of our souls and bodies and that he may be the center of our affections even as he was for Mary and Joseph.
Finally, O Lord, may sin never disturb our union on earth.
May we be eternally united in heaven with you and Mary and Joseph and all your saints. Amen.

# A Wife's Prayer for Her Husband

Jesus Lord, my heart is for my husband.
It is he whom I love and for whom I pray now.
Help me to learn what is for his happiness and our mutual love.
Help me to touch his heart and to bring joy to his life.
May we truly rejoice in each other, share our plans and wishes, and care for each others needs.
Help us always to make our lives grow in maturity, grace, and the wisdom of your revelation.
Lord Jesus, in your providence we are together.
Help us to appreciate this great gift.
Amen.

# A Husband's Prayer for His Wife

Lord Jesus, in the heart of my heart you know my desire is for my wife's happiness.

You know also I want her to share her love with me and I want to share my love with her.

May the good grace of your Spirit guide my uncertain ways that I may be the instrument of my wife's happiness.

Help me to express my love in big and little ways.

Help us to rejoice in each other, to be helpful and thoughtful, always to be aware of the mystery of each others personality.

I believe we are joined to each other in you.

Show us your favor, Lord Jesus. Amen.

## Prayer for a Man Deceased

Incline your ear, O Lord, to our prayers in which we humbly pray that you show your mercy to the soul of your servant (N...), whom you commanded to leave this world.
Place him in the region of peace and light and bid him share the company of your saints.
Through Christ our Lord. Amen.

## Prayer for a Woman Deceased

O Lord, we beg of you, through your loving kindness, have mercy on the soul of your servant (N...), and now that she is set free from the defilements of this mortal flesh, restore her to her heritage of everlasting salvation.
Through Christ our Lord. Amen.

## For a Deceased Spouse

O heavenly Father, I am now in the shadow of great loneliness.

My helpmate has been taken from me.

Yet I submit in holy faith to your divine will.

I know that you love my spouse who, I pray, is now in heaven rejoicing with you.

Grant me the strength I need to bear my present burdens, and help me to look for opportunities to seek out those less fortunate than myself.

Keep me from feeling sorry for myself in my present condition, and keep my heart enflamed with love for you and for my neighbor, so that I can help to carry on your work of love in this world.

May I one day be re-united with my beloved spouse in heaven, where we both can worship you for all eternity. Amen.

## Prayer for Deceased Priests

O heavenly Father, Father of the great high priest, your Son, Jesus Christ, we pray for the happy repose of all deceased priests.
These men gave their lives to bring the love of your Son to the world.
Look kindly on them and give them a share of your glory in heaven.
We ask this in the name of your Son, Jesus, our Lord. Amen.

## Prayer for the Faithful Departed

Eternal rest grant unto them, O Lord.
Response: And let perpetual light shine upon them.
May their souls and the souls of all the faithful departed through the mercy of God rest in peace. Amen.

## Act of Resignation to the Divine Will

O Lord, my God, I, now at this moment, readily and willingly accept at Your hand whatever kind of death it may please You to send me, with all its pains, penalties and sorrows. Amen.

## Prayer for a Happy Death

Lord Jesus, by your agony and death, deliver me from a sudden and unexpected death.

I humbly beseech you to never let me die unexpectedly and pass from this life without the Sacraments.

Jesus, my Lord, by all your labors and sorrows, by your precious Blood and most holy wounds, and by your words on the cross: "My God, My God, why hast Thou forsaken me?" and again: "Father, into Thy hands I commend my spirit", I beseech you to save me from an unexpected death.

Give me, most merciful Jesus, time for penance; and pray that I may pass from this life happily into your grace, that I may love you with my whole heart, and bless you for ever and ever. Amen.

## Prayer for Vocations

O Lord Jesus Christ,
 strength of those who leave all things
 and follow you, raise up, we beg you,
 the vocations which the Church needs.
 Help our young boys to understand
 the happiness which comes to the priest
 as he carries on the work of Christ
 and brings God himself to the altar
 for man.
 Inspire them with a burning desire
 to share in this priesthood.
Call other young men
 to our brotherhoods, where in the
 holy life of religious communities
 they may imitate your virtues,
 carry on the educational, charitable

and apostolic works of your Church
and travel toward eternal bliss.
Give us, dear Lord,
zealous and apostolic priests,
dedicated and self-sacrificing
religious, brothers and sisters.
Bless us abundantly with workers who
will generously spend themselves
for the restoration of all things in you
and the glorification of
your heavenly Father, who, with you
and the Holy Spirit, lives and reigns,
for ever and ever. Amen.

# Prayers of the Saints

# The Magnificat

My soul proclaims the greatness
  of the Lord and my spirit
  exults in God my saviour;
  because he has looked upon his
  lowly handmaid.
Yes, from this day forward
  all generations will call me blessed,
  for the Almighty
  has done great things for me.
Holy is his name, and his mercy reaches
  from age to age
  for those who fear him.
He has shown the power of his arm,
  he has routed the proud of heart.
He has pulled down princes
  from their thrones and
  exalted the lowly.
The hungry he has filled with good
  things, the rich sent empty away.
He has come to the help of Israel
  his servant, mindful of his mercy—
  according to the promise he made
  to our ancestors— of his mercy to
  Abraham and to his descendants
  for ever. *Mary, Mother of Jesus*

Lord, make me an instrument of your peace.
> where there is hatred, let me sow love;
> where there is injury, pardon;
> where there is doubt, faith;
> where there is despair, hope;
> where there is darkness, light;
> and where there is sadness, joy.

O Divine Master, grant that I may not so much seek to be consoled as to console,
> to be understood as to understand,
> to be loved as to love.

For it is in giving that we receive,
> it is in pardoning
> that we are pardoned,
> and it is in dying
> that we are born to eternal life.

*St. Francis of Assisi*

Breathe in me, Holy Spirit, that all my
   thoughts may be holy.
Act in me, Holy Spirit, that my work
   too may be holy.
Draw my heart, Holy Spirit, that I may
   love only what is holy.
Strengthen me, Holy Spirit, to defend
   all that is holy.
Guard me, Holy Spirit, that I may always be holy.
*St. Augustine*

Lord, I am willing to be poor in all those
   things of which I have been deprived
   as I am ready to be rich, O Lord,
   if it be your will and to your glory;
   not my will according to nature,
   O Lord, but your will and
   my will according to spirit be done.
*Bl. Jan Van Ruysbroeck*

From eternity to eternity,
   you are my God.
All shall perish and pass away,
   but you remain for ever.
*St. Elizabeth Ann Seton*

O God, you are my God,
  in you will I hope!
You will be my help and my refuge.
I shall not fear,
  for not only are you with me
  but you are in me and I in you.

*St. Francis de Sales*


O my God, I beg of you to grant me
  peace with my neighbor,
  for I cannot enjoy your favor
  if I do not live in union
  with my brothers and sisters.
I can preserve this union by mildness
  and patience.
Give me, then, I beseech you,
  these two virtues, and
  grant that I may always speak and act
  kindly to all;
  that I may suffer patiently
  for love of you whatever wrongs,
  injuries, or insults may be done me;
  that not only I may not be angered
  or displeased with anything but
  that I may patiently suffer all
  that happens to me from others.

*St. John Baptist de La Salle*

Teach us, good Lord,
   to serve you as you deserve:
   to give and not to count the cost;
   to fight and not to heed the wounds;
   to toil and not to seek for rest;
   to labor and not ask for any reward
   save that of knowing that we do
   your will.

*St. Ignatius Loyola*

Behold me, O my God,
   I give myself to you,
   to your good pleasure.
Because I love you, I will give you
   the homage of submitting
   my whole being to your will,
   whatever it may be.

*Columba Marmion*

Good Lord, give me the grace
   so to spend my life, that
   when the day of my death shall come,
   though I feel pain in my body,
   I may feel comfort in soul;
   and with faithful hope of your mercy,
   in due love towards you and
   charity towards the world, I may,

through your grace,
part hence into your glory.
*St. Thomas More*

O Lord, endow me with more
contentedness in what is present, and
less solicitude about what is future;
with a patient mind to submit
to any loss of what I have, or to any
disappointment of what I expect.
*Simon Patrick*

Have mercy on me:
  I am a sinner, I am weak.
Be gracious, O God, to my weakness;
  grant strength to me to pray a prayer
  that will be pleasing to your will.
*St. Ephrem the Syrian*

Grant me, O Lord my God,
  a mind to know you,
  a heart to seek you,
  wisdom to find you,
  conduct pleasing to you,
  faithful perseverance in waiting for you
  and a hope of finally embracing you.
*St. Thomas Aquinas*

O my God, I ask of you for myself and for those whom I hold dear, the grace to fulfill perfectly your holy will, to accept for love of you the joys and sorrows of this passing life, so that we may one day be united in Heaven for all eternity.

*St. Theresa of Lisieux*

Christ, as a light,
  illumine and guide me!
Christ, as a shield, o'ershadow
  and cover me!
Christ, be under me! Christ,
  be over me!
Christ, be beside me,
  on left hand and right!
Christ, this day be within
  and without me!
Christ, the lowly and meek,
Christ, the all-powerful,
Be in the heart of each
  to whom I speak-
In the mouth of each
  who speaks to me-
In all who draw near to me,
  or see me, or hear me!

*St. Patrick*

# The Universal Prayer

Lord, I believe in you:
  increase my faith.
I trust in you: strengthen my trust.
I love you:
  let me love you more and more.
I am sorry for my sins:
  deepen my sorrow.
I worship you as my first beginning,
  I long for you as my last end,
  I praise you as my constant helper,
  and call on you as my loving protector.
Guide me by your wisdom,
  correct me with your justice,
  comfort me with your mercy,
  protect me with your power.
I offer you, Lord, my thoughts:
  to be fixed on you;
  my words: to have you for their theme;
  my actions: to reflect my love for you;
  my sufferings: to be endured
  for your greater glory.
I want to do what you ask of me:
  in the way you ask,
  for as long as you ask,
  because you ask it.

Lord, enlighten my understanding,
  strengthen my will,
  purify my heart,
  and make me holy.
Help me to repent of my past sins
  and to resist temptation in the future.
Help me to rise above my human weaknesses and to grow stronger as a Christian.
Let me love you, my Lord and my God,
  and see myself as I really am:
  a pilgrim in this world,
  a Christian called to respect and love all whose lives I touch,
  those in authority over me
  or those under my authority,
  my friends and my enemies.
Help me to conquer anger with gentleness, greed by generosity,
  apathy by fervor.
Help me to forget myself
  and reach out toward others.
Make me prudent in planning,
  courageous in taking risks.
Make me patient in suffering,
  unassuming in prosperity.

Keep me, Lord, attentive at prayer,
   temperate in food and drink,
   diligent in my work,
   firm in my good intentions.
Let my conscience be clear,
   my conduct without fault,
   my speech blameless,
   my life well-ordered.
Put me on guard against my human
   weaknesses.
Let me cherish your love for me,
   keep your law, and come at last
   to your salvation.
Teach me to realize that this world is
   passing, that my true future is the
   happiness of heaven, that life on
   earth is short, and the life to come
   eternal.
Help me to prepare for death
   with a proper fear of judgment,
   but a greater trust in your goodness.
Lead me safely through death to the
   endless joy of heaven.
Grant this through Christ our Lord.
   Amen.

*Pope Clement XI*

# Prayer of the Heart

IN RECENT YEARS there has been great interest in what is known as centering prayer or Prayer of the Heart. Prayer essentially is "personal communication with the Lord" and centering prayer is a way of experiencing God in the very depths of our being.

Thomas Merton, the late Trappist monk, focused attention on this form of prayer in much of his spiritual writing and reflection. From ancient times to the present, the descent into one's deepest self to seek the presence of God has been a rewarding spiritual experience.

In today's complex style of living, with its accompanying tensions, more people are finding this form of meditation, Prayer of the Heart, to be especially helpful. To communicate with God in this manner, the following steps are recommended:

A. Choose a place where you can be alone without distraction. Take a comfortable bodily position, close your eyes and put everything out of your mind.

B. Physically relax and let all tensions leave you. Deep, deliberate breathing will aid this process. Let your total being, mind and body, arrive at a gentle silence.

C. Center all your attention on God and let a word or phrase form in your consciousness. You may use "Jesus" or "Jesus, have mercy" or "Come Holy Spirit" or whatever else will relate you to the Lord.

D. The word or phrase may be repeated often or interspersed with periods of complete silence. This is your way of reaching out for and receiving the Lord.

E. Your prayer should end slowly and quietly. You may wish to recite an Our Father or Hail Mary with great deliberation. On occasion the Lord may invite you to a deeper silence or listening and you will come to know the joy of his Spirit in fullest measure.